Hermeneutics and the Rhetorical Tradition

Chapters in the Ancient Legacy & Its Humanist Reception

KATHY EDEN

Yale University Press   *New Haven and London*

Designed by Sonia L. Scanlon
Set in Fournier type by The Marathon Group, Inc.,
Durham, North Carolina.
Printed in the United States of America by Edwards Brothers,
Inc., Ann Arbor, Michigan.

Library of Congress Cataloging-in-Publication Data
Eden, Kathy, 1952–
Hermeneutics and the rhetorical tradition : chapters in the
ancient legacy and its humanist reception / Kathy Eden.
    p.   cm. — (Yale studies in hermeneutics)
Includes bibliographical references and index.
ISBN 0-300-06694-5 (cloth : alk. paper)
1. Hermeneutics—History.   2. Rhetoric—History.   I. Title.
II. Series.
BD241.E34   1997
121'.68—dc20   96-28635
                CIP

A catalogue record for this book is available from
the British Library.
The paper in this book meets the guidelines for permanence and
durability of the Committee on Production Guidelines for Book
Longevity of the Council on Library Resources.

10 9 8 7 6 5 4 3 2 1

οἰκείοις καὶ φίλοις

Emma Eden Ramos
Anna Eden Ramos
Carey Richard Ramos

Contents

Acknowledgments

Over the past ten years, my engagement with the material that makes up this book has been enriched by conversations with colleagues, students, and friends. Thanks are due to Teodolinda Barolini, James Biester, Caroline Bynum, Mary Carruthers, Rita Copeland, Robert Ferguson, Helene Foley, Pierre Force, Eileen Gillooly, Moshe Gold, Patricia Grieve, Robert Hanning, Rebeca Helfer, Donald Kelley, Richard Kuhns, Dirk Obbink, Wesley Trimpi, and Ann Van Sant. Its final form owes a special debt to the critical readings of Anthony Grafton and Joel Weinsheimer.

Introduction

In 1515 Erasmus pens his well-known letter to Martin Dorp concerning the objections of a group of theologians to his controversial but immensely popular *Praise of Folly*. In Folly's defense, Erasmus aggressively prosecutes her detractors, attacking in particular their interpretive practices. They are the sort of readers, he alleges, who "choose out a few statements from a long work" (*propositiones aliquot eligant ex magno decerptas opere;* Allen, 2:106; *CWE*, 3:130), the sort who "take a couple of words out of their context (*duo verba decerpere*), sometimes a little altered in the process, leaving out everything that softens (*leniunt*) and explains (*explicant*) what sounds harsh otherwise" (Allen, 2:102; *CWE*, 3:126).[1]

Laying bare the interpretive methods of these detractors, Erasmus, in good humanist fashion, also locates their ancient sources: "Quintilian picks up this trick in his *Institutio* and shows us how to play it: we recount our own story in the most flattering light, with supporting evidence and anything else that can mitigate (*mitiget*) or extenuate (*extenuet*) or help our case in any way; we should recite our opponent's case, on the other hand, shorn of all this assistance in the most invidious language it allows of " (Allen, 2:102; *CWE*, 3:126). Here Erasmus probably has in mind Quintilian's advice to the orator on refuting an opponent's arguments in court (*Institutio Oratoria* 5.13.25–28). In a general way, Erasmus's reliance on

---

1. For the letters of Erasmus I have used *Opus epistolarum Des. Erasmi Roterodami*, edited by P. S. Allen, H. M. Allen, H. W. Garrod, 11 vols. (Oxford, 1906–58), cited hereafter as Allen, and *The Correspondence of Erasmus*, translated by R. A. B. Mynors and D. F. S. Thomson, in *The Collected Works of Erasmus*, 86 vols. projected (Toronto, 1974–), cited hereafter as *CWE*. For an introduction to the debate with Dorp, see *The Complete Works of St. Thomas More*, vol. 15, edited by Daniel Kinney (New Haven, 1986), xix–xlv, and Erika Rummel, *Erasmus and His Catholic Critics*, vol. 1 (Nieuwkoop, 1989), 1–13.

Quintilian's authority to bolster his defense draws our attention to the larger rhetorical context of the early history of hermeneutics. As practiced by the ancients and their humanist admirers, interpretation is by and large adversarial, an antagonistic affair. Because one of its most pressing arenas was the law courts, moreover, many of its most compelling strategies belong to forensic debate.

Indeed, the most comprehensive and detailed treatments of interpretation in so-called classical antiquity come from the rhetorical manuals of Cicero and Quintilian, among others, and more particularly from their treatments of *interpretatio scripti*, the interpretation of written material pertinent to legal cases, such as laws, wills, and contracts. In the course of these treatments, as we will see, rhetoricians—and the grammarians who shared large portions of their curriculum—considered such seemingly current hermeneutical questions as the nature of meaning and the role of context in the quest for this meaning. Expert in the art of accommodation, as the *ars rhetorica* was frequently called, they also recognized the accommodative nature of all interpretation founded upon this same art.

As glimpsed in his polemic against Folly's detractors, Erasmian hermeneutics is arguably the most influential and certainly the best known humanist rehabilitation of this ancient tradition. The measure of recovery, however, is reflected less in Erasmus's outspoken allegiance to Quintilian than in his more tacit identification of the best kind of interpretation with equity. For the ancient rhetoricians, as we shall see, routinely elaborated the principles of interpretation alongside the arguments for an equitable judgment, where equity (Gr. *epieikeia*, Lat. *aequitas*) was understood as the mitigating corrective to the generality and consequent rigidity inherent in the law. Designed, in contrast to legal statute, as a flexible measure, equity could take into account the infinite particularity of human events by investigating the agents' intentions and thus could accommodate each individual case.

So Erasmus in his letter to Dorp calls for a method of reading that, like equity, softens or mitigates the text it explains, substituting, as it were, friendly and familiar terms—*commoda verba* (Allen, 2:104)—for the sometimes alien and unsettling expression of the original. Interpretation of this kind draws the reader's attention away from the words themselves to the writer's intention. Surely, Erasmus argues by way of illustration (Allen,

2:104), the holy *scriptor* would not be taken at his word in calling Christ a grave-robber, an adulterer, or a drunkard. Why then, he asks, should his *Folly* be interpreted any less equitably: "Give me a prejudiced interpreter to put a brief and invidious explanation on this, and what could sound more intolerable? Let a pious (*pius*) and fair-minded (*aequus*) man read what I wrote, and he will find the allegory (*allegoriam*) acceptable" (Allen, 2:104; *CWE*, 3:128). Here, as elsewhere in this letter and throughout his hermeneutical writings (for example, Allen, 2:105), Erasmus applauds the equitable interpreter, the *interpres aequus*, for his method of reading. In contrast to that practiced by Folly's detractors, this kind of interpretation accommodates the meaning of the words to the speaker's meaning, the letter (*littera*) to the spirit (*spiritus*).

Indeed, Erasmus's identification of equitable and spiritual interpretation reflects a complex set of accommodations with far-reaching consequences for the early history of hermeneutics. It provides, we might say, one especially striking instance of old wine in new bottles. For centuries earlier, as we shall see, the same first Fathers of the Church who occupy so much of Erasmus's rhetorical, grammatical, and theological attention transform the relation between strict law and equity from classical legal theory into one between the Old Dispensation under Jewish law and a New Dispensation of the Spirit under Jesus Christ. Rejecting the "literalizing" practices of their so-called Judaizing forebears, these early Christians advocate instead a spiritual reading of Scripture. They do so, however, without simply identifying this kind of reading with allegorical interpretation, associated in its extreme forms and excessive application with pagan, especially Greek, philosophy. Thus accommodating a double inheritance, patristic exegesis labors not only to "domesticate" but even to "bring into one and the same household" their not always compatible Jewish and Hellenistic relations. The humanist offspring of this exegetical theory, in turn, looks to rediscover the various lines of descent among its oldest ancestors.

The itinerary within the rhetorical tradition from equitable to spiritual and back to equitable interpretation, then, represents, as it were, a returning home; and this metaphor of "homecoming," as we shall also see, proves especially apt for the hermeneutical tradition here considered. For "accommodation" (Gr. *sunoikeioun*, Lat. *accommodare*), the process so crucial to rhetorical production and interpretation, includes in its radical sense the act of "making to feel like one of the family." Advocating the *commoda verba*, or "familiar words," of Erasmus's method, this tradition, without forfeiting the tensions inherent in its adversarial origins, thematizes the interpretive act, at its best, as the arduous journey home.

Like the analogy between reading and homecoming, the relation between rhetoric and hermeneutics will be familiar to students of interpretation-theory from several quarters. One is the modern discipline of hermeneutics, now roughly two centuries old, that looks back to Friedrich Schleiermacher as its progenitor and Protestant Germany as its fatherland. Throughout his lectures, Schleiermacher, devoted to the study of antiquity, claims universality for the unity of hermeneutics and rhetoric because "every act of understanding is the obverse of an act of discourse, in that one must come to grasp the thought that was at the base of the discourse."[2] Another is the hermeneutics of the earliest Protestants, also students of antiquity. Martin Luther, arguably Schleiermacher's most adversarial (and certainly his most rhetorically effective) forefather, insists in a telling mixture of Latin and the vernacular that Scripture is not understood unless it is "brought home (*zu haus*), that is experienced (*experiatur*)."[3] Yet a third is the philosophical hermeneutics of the past fifty years, chiefly associated with the work of Hans-Georg Gadamer.

Recently characterized as a secular Luther,[4] Gadamer, who began his academic career in classical philology, reaffirms Schleiermacher's insight that (in Gadamer's words) "the rhetorical and hermeneutical aspects of human linguisticality completely interpenetrate each other."[5] In his magnum opus, *Truth and Method*, this insight receives full attention. There, Gadamer not only reminds us of the ancient rhetorical origins of both the

2. "*The Hermeneutics:* Outline of the 1819 Lectures," 4.2, translated by Jan Wojcik and Roland Haas, *New Literary History* 10 (1978): 1–16.

3. *Dr Martin Luthers Tischreden (1531–46)*, vol. 3 (Weimar, 1914), 170, quoted by Gerald L. Bruns, *Hermeneutics Ancient and Modern* (New Haven, 1992), 147.

4. See Bruns, *Hermeneutics Ancient and Modern*, 158.

5. "On the Scope and Function of Hermeneutical Reflection," translated by G. B. Hess and R. E. Palmer, in *Philosophical Hermeneutics*, edited by David E. Linge (Berkeley, 1976), 25.

hermeneutic circle and the concept of hermeneutical application, especially in the workings of Aristotelian equity, but he also locates all hermeneutical activity between two extremes: the strange or foreign, at one pole, and the familiar, at the other, where familiarity retains its radical sense of belonging to one's home.[6] Indeed, the reader experiences reading *Truth and Method* as an odyssey through the alien terrain of past understandings of understanding; and like the *Odyssey,* this intellectual journey home requires scenes of discovery—most especially, the reader's recognition that the understanding of others belongs somehow to one's own understanding, not only of the past but of oneself.

Finally, students of interpretation-theory are likely to have encountered aspects of the broader relations detailed in the following chapters in historical studies of hermeneutics, some dealing with the contributions of individuals or groups of individuals, some with whole periods and traditions.[7] As subsequent footnotes will reveal, this book is indebted to many of these studies. At the same time, it takes as its peculiar point of departure the model of reading grounded in *interpretatio scripti,* an element of the ancient rhetorical art rarely mentioned as the *fons et origo* of

6. See Hans-Georg Gadamer, *Truth and Method,* translated by Joel Weinsheimer and Donald G. Marshall (New York, 1989), esp. 190, 291–93, 295, 317–24. See also Gadamer, "Rhetorik und Hermeneutik," in *Gesammelte Werke,* vol. 2 (Tübingen, 1986), 276–91, and "*Logos* and *Ergon* in Plato's *Lysis,*" in *Dialogue and Dialectic: Eight Hermeneutical Studies on Plato,* translated by P. Christopher Smith (New Haven, 1980), 18–19. And see Joel Weinsheimer, *Philosophical Hermeneutics and Literary Theory* (New Haven, 1991), 69–86.

7. The bibliography in each of these categories is substantial. For purposes of illustration, consider, on a single figure, Manfred Hoffman, *Rhetoric and Theology: The Hermeneutic of Erasmus* (Toronto, 1994); on a group of individuals, Werner Alexander, *Hermeneutica Generalis: Zur Konzeption und Entwicklung der allgemeinem Verstehenslehre im 17 und 18 Jahrhundert* (Stuttgart, 1993); for whole traditions, Rita Copeland, *Rhetoric, Hermeneutics and Translation in the Middle Ages: Academic Traditions and Vernacular Texts* (Cambridge, 1991), Michael J. Hyde and Craig Smith, "Hermeneutics and Rhetoric: A Seen but Unobserved Relationship," *Quarterly Journal of Speech* 65 (1979): 347–63, and Glenn W. Most, "Rhetorik und Hermeneutik: Zur Konstitution der Neuzeitlichkeit," *Antike und Abendland* 30 (1984): 62–79. See also two recent volumes on the relation between rhetoric and hermeneutics: *Reconfiguring the Relation Rhetoric/Hermeneutics,* edited by George Pullman, *Studies in the Literary Imagination,* 28 (1995), and *Rhetoric and Hermeneutics in Our Time,* edited by Walter Jost and Michael J. Hyde (New Haven, 1997).

these broader relations. As I shall argue, however, this element of the rhetorical tradition plays a key role in the development of two critical phases of the early history (or what one recent historian has called the "prehistory")[8] of hermeneutics. Apart from this model of reading, patristic and humanist hermeneutics, often credited with prefiguring the later hermeneutical tradition, are unthinkable.

8. See Jean Grondin, *Introduction to Philosophical Hermeneutics,* translated by Joel Weinsheimer (New Haven, 1994), ch. 1, "On the Prehistory of Hermeneutics," 17–44.

CHAPTER ONE

Hermeneutics and Ancient Rhetoric

Interpretatio scripti

As beneficiaries of the Hellenistic rhetorical tradition, once comprehensive but now almost completely lost, Roman rhetoricians inherit, as part of their larger legacy, a loosely organized set of rules for interpreting the written materials pertinent to legal cases, such as laws, wills, and contracts—what contemporary American lawyers might call the rules of documentary construction and what at least one especially influential Roman lawyer calls *interpretatio scripti*.[1] Throughout his rhetorical treatises, Cicero formulates and reformulates these rules as part of his legal and rhetorical theory. As this book will argue, these formulations belong to a dominant strand of hermeneutical reflection that continues to shape interpretation-theory long after the last performance of the last ancient orator. While subsequent chapters will trace the influence of these rules on ancient grammarians, early Church Fathers, and Renaissance humanists, this first chapter will look to establish the Ciceronian contribution, both as gradually developed by Cicero himself and as received and transmitted by his most influential ancient admirer, Quintilian.

In his mature works, as part of a general rethinking of his rhetorical theory, Cicero revises his views on interpretation. His major revision concerns the number of controversies that can arise over disputed texts. Whereas the early *De inventione*, which preserves the fullest discussion of *interpretatio scripti* (2.40.116–2.51.154), numbers the controversies at five,

---

1. See A. Arthur Schiller, "Roman Interpretatio and Anglo-American Interpretation and Construction," *Virginia Law Review* 27 (1941): 735–68; Robert Dick Sider, *Ancient Rhetoric and the Art of Tertullian* (Oxford, 1971), esp. 85ff.; and Kathy Eden, "Hermeneutics and the Ancient Rhetorical Tradition," *Rhetorica* 5 (1987): 59–86.

the later works, including the *De oratore*, *Orator*, and *Topica*, reduce that number to three (*De oratore* 1.31.140, 2.26.110; *Topica* 95–96). Folding into the three remaining grounds both analogy (*ratiocinatio*) and definition (*definitio, vis verbi*) (*De inventione* 2.40.116; cf. 1.13.17–18), these later works preserve from the earlier treatment (1) the discrepancy between the written words and the writer's intention, routinely formulated as either *scriptum* versus *voluntas* or *scriptum* versus *sententia*, (2) ambiguity (Lat. *ambiguitas*), either in a word or passage, and (3) contradiction (Lat. *ex contrariis legibus*), either within a single text or between two related texts, such as two laws.[2]

Cicero's understanding of interpretation in terms of controversy—indeed, his inclusion of interpretation-theory in rhetorical theory—is decisive for the history of hermeneutics, not because he is the first theorist to do so but because his works enjoy the widest reception. And for Cicero, rhetoric in its broadest sense is the art of persuasion, rooted in a procedure called *disputatio in utramque partem*, argument on either side of the question. Both the student in training, in the exercises known as declamations, and the experienced lawyer, in preparing an actual case, work through all the grounds *for* and *against* the defendant, continually refining their strategies for making and overturning the same arguments.[3] As part of the rhetorical art, interpretation shares this procedure.

Whereas the *De oratore* remarks in passing that every schoolboy knows how to counter an argument for *scriptum* with one for *voluntas* (*De oratore* 1.57.244), the *De inventione*, as a manual for just such a schoolboy, lays out these arguments in full detail, recommending in particular the strategy of coopting the adversary's position. Thus the advocate of *scriptum* should insist that he and not his opponent really upholds the *scriptor*'s *voluntas* by

2. Nearly contemporary with the *De inventione*, the *Ad Herennium* lists six grounds of controversy, adding *translatio* (Gr. *metalēpsis*) to the five of Cicero's early treatise (1.11.19–1.14.24). On the opposition between *scriptum* and *voluntas* in the ancient rhetorical treatises, see Heinrich Lausberg, *Handbuch der Literarischen Rhetorik* (Munich, 1960), 118–19, and Wesley Trimpi, *Muses of One Mind: The Literary Analysis of Experience and Its Continuity* (Princeton, 1983), 278–82. For a different set of hermeneutical principles operative in ancient law, see Donald R. Kelley, "Gaius Noster: Substructures of Western Social Thought," *American Historical Review* 84 (1979): 619–48.

3. See S. F. Bonner, *Roman Declamation in the Late Republic and Early Empire* (Liverpool, 1949), and *Education in Ancient Rome* (Berkeley, 1977), and Trimpi, *Muses of One Mind*, 285–327.

respecting the words that preserve it (2.44.128). The advocate of *voluntas*, in turn, should find some way either to get *scriptum* on his side or, alternatively, to undercut the assumed clarity of the disputed document, shifting the ground of controversy from *scriptum/voluntas* to ambiguity: "the speaker who opposes the letter (*contra scriptum*) will profit greatly by converting something in the written document (*ex ipsa scriptura*) to his own case or by showing that it contains some ambiguity; then on the basis of that ambiguity he may defend the passage which helps his case . . . because if he can remove the foundation on which his opponent's case rests, he will lessen and mitigate all its force and effectiveness" (2.48.142–43; cf. Quintilian 7.6.5–12).[4] Sometimes, then, the grounds of controversy will overlap, as a debate over words and intention shifts to a debate over the meaning of the words. At other times, a contradiction between two laws may be resolved with the help of one of the other two grounds, insofar as the law free from ambiguity or a discrepancy between the words and the intention arguably takes precedence over the law subject to further controversy (*De inventione* 2.49.147; cf. *Orator* 121).

In spite of both inevitable overlapping and respectable precedent in the rhetorical tradition, Cicero, followed by Quintilian, rejects further conflation of these grounds. In theory, if not always in practice, Quintilian contends, they are and must remain distinct:

> The *basis* concerned with the *letter* and the *intention*
> of the law involves a legal question as regards the
> interpretation of the words, which is identical with
> the question arising out of *contrary laws*. Conse-
> quently some writers have asserted that all these *bases*
> may be resolved into those concerned with the *letter*
> and *intention*, while others hold that in all cases where
> the *letter* and the *intention* of a document have to be
> considered, it is *ambiguity* that gives rise to the ques-
> tion at issue. But all these *bases* are really distinct, for

4. Cicero, *De inventione,* translated by H. M. Hubbell, Loeb Classical Library (London, 1949). Unless otherwise indicated, all references are to this edition. For a general introduction to this early manual, see George Kennedy, *The Art of Rhetoric in the Roman World* (Princeton, 1972), 103–48.

an obscure point of law is not the same as an ambiguous point of law. [7.10.2][5]

Indeed, Quintilian's insistence on safeguarding distinctions between the kinds of controversy in *interpretatio scripti,* and especially between *scriptum/voluntas* and ambiguity, points to an even more profound division fundamental to the treatment of rhetorical material—a division reflected not only in the ubiquitous opposition between *res* and *verba* but also in the traditional separation in the manuals of matters of proof (Gr. *pistis,* Lat. *probatio*) from matters of style (Gr. *lexis,* Lat. *elocutio*). Aristotle's *Rhetoric,* the anonymous *Ad Herennium,* Cicero's *De oratore,* and Quintilian's *Institutio Oratoria,* to cite a few examples, all turn to matters of style only after treating matters of proof, a priority reflected equally in the traditional ordering of the five rhetorical *partes,* with invention in first place and elocution in third.

This deep and enduring division in the arts of rhetoric has far-reaching consequences for interpretation. Whereas the first ground of controversy, the discrepancy between the writer's words and his intention, borrows its principles from the rhetorical treatments of proof, based on a fundamentally legal model, ambiguity, the second ground of controversy, receives its fullest articulation in the treatments of style.[6] Further in keeping with this split, each of the separate divisions of the art enforces its own theory of meaning, which by turns complements and confounds that of the other. The arts of rhetoric, in other words, characterize meaning differently in their different sections: under invention as intentionality—what moral and legal agents mean to do or say—and under elocution as signification— what words mean. In those parts of the manuals covering *interpretatio scripti,* these two concepts of meaning collide, engendering not only the overlap between the first and second grounds of controversy but also the

5. Quintilian, *Institutio Oratoria,* translated by H. E. Butler, 4 vols., Loeb Classical Library (London, 1921), hereafter cited as Quintilian. Unless otherwise indicated, all references are to this edition.

6. For the traditional division in the rhetorical manuals between matters of proof and matters of style, see Friedrich Solmsen, "The Aristotelian Tradition in Ancient Rhetoric," *American Journal of Philology* 62 (1941): 35–50, 169–90. For the origins of rhetoric in forensic oratory, see Quintilian 3.2.2, and Kathy Eden, *Poetic and Legal Fiction in the Aristotelian Tradition* (Princeton, 1986), 9–19.

competing claims of *voluntas* and *scriptum*. The history of this collision, moreover, coincides with the history of rhetorical theory.

As the father of what Cicero calls the *mos Aristotelius* (*De oratore* 3.21.80), another term describing the procedure of arguing on either side of a question, Aristotle not only draws attention to the place of written documents, such as laws and contracts, in legal argument, but he also recommends strategies for using these documents to one's advantage, including the manipulation of contradictions and ambiguities (*Rhetoric* 1.15.3–12; 3.15.9–10). The advocate presented in court with a law prejudicial to his case is advised to argue against strict construction in favor of equity, for equity upholds not only the defendant's intention (*prohairēsis*) over his action (*praxis*) but also the legislator's intention (*dianoia*) over his words (*logos*) (1.13.17).[7] Preserved in subsequent Greek manuals, as Quintilian reminds us (3.6.46; cf. 3.6.60–62), as *rhēton* versus *dianoia*, the discrepancy between the writer's words and intention figures in legal argumentation in the oldest extant treatment of the rhetorical art.[8]

Whereas Aristotle treats intentionality, a principle fundamental to his rhetorical, legal, and, more broadly, ethical theory, in the first of the three books of his *Rhetoric*, he delays his full treatment of ambiguity (Gr. *amphibolia*) until the third (3.2.13, 3.5.4–5, 3.18.5), as part of a more comprehensive treatment of style.[9] Relying on discussions elsewhere, especially the *Poetics* and *Topics*, the *Rhetoric* reflects a theory of language and advances a theory of style rooted in the recognition that words signify in more than one way (*posachōs sēmainein*) (cf. *Rhetoric* 2.23.9; *Poetics* 25.22; and *Topics* 1.15).[10] Indeed, multiple signification lies at the root not only of

7. For the crucial role of equity in Aristotle's ethical, legal, and poetic theory, see Eden, *Poetic and Legal Fiction in the Aristotelian Tradition*, 25–61. For the distinction between *prohairēsis* and *dianoia*, see *Rhetoric* 3.16.9; A. M. Dale, "Ethos and Dianoia: 'Character' and 'Thought' in Aristotle's *Poetics*," in *Collected Papers* (Cambridge, 1969), 139–55; and Eden, "Hermeneutics and the Ancient Rhetorical Tradition," 71–72.

8. On *voluntas* as a translation of *dianoia*, see Albrecht Dihle, *The Theory of Will in Classical Antiquity* (Berkeley, 1982), 135–38, 241–42, and Lausberg, *Handbuch der Literarischen Rhetorik*, 109, 118.

9. For Aristotle on style, see Eden, "Hermeneutics and the Ancient Rhetorical Tradition," 73–75, and Stephen Halliwell, *Aristotle's Poetics* (Chapel Hill, 1986), 344–49. See also William Bedell Stanford, *Ambiguity in Greek Literature* (Oxford, 1939), esp. 5–68.

10. I consider the relevant chapters of the *Poetics* in the following chapter. See also the first four chapters of *On Interpretation* and T. H. Irwin, "Aristotle's Concept of Signification,"

such indispensable instruments of expression as metaphor, to which I shall return in chapter 2, but also of such vices of style as ambiguity. Whereas metaphor manipulates this multiple signification to effect greater vividness and especially clarity, the principal virtue of style (cf. *Rhetoric* 3.2.8–3.44), ambiguity is vicious because it results in obscurity.[11]

Following Aristotle, Cicero considers ambiguity a feature of style, one rooted in multiple signification. Although resisting an extended treatment of this stylistic feature (in keeping with its focus on invention), the *De inventione* nevertheless addresses the problem of ambiguity as a part of its consideration of *interpretatio scripti*. A controversy arises from ambiguity, Cicero explains, when what the writer *meant* is obscure because the written statement has two or more *meanings* or significations (*ex ambiguo autem nascitur controversia cum quid senserit scriptor obscurum est, quod scriptum duas pluresve res significat*) (2.40.116; cf. 1.13.17). The *De oratore*, in contrast, investigates ambiguity in some detail, identifying it specifically as an element of *verba* rather than *res* (2.26.110–112, 2.61.250–2.65.261; cf. *Orator* 121).

Quintilian follows Cicero on this matter, not only adducing certain philosophers who hold that "there is not a single word which does not have a diversity of meanings" (*nullum videatur esse verbum quod non plura significet*) (7.9.1) but also postponing a thorough treatment of ambiguity, the principal vice of style, until Book 8, the first of the two consecutive books of the *Institutio* concerned specifically with elocution or style (8 Proem 13; cf. 8.2.16–21). As a ground of controversy, moreover, ambiguity further differs from *scriptum/voluntas* in that it always raises the conjectural *status* or question, whereas *scriptum/voluntas* more often turns on the issue of quality, the *status qualitatis* (3.6.43, 3.6.87–89); and the link between the argument for intention and the qualitative *basis* or *status* is equity (cf.

---

in *Language and Logos: Studies in Ancient Greek Philosophy Presented to G. E. L. Owen*, edited by Malcolm Schofield and Martha Craven Nussbaum (Cambridge, 1982), 241–66; K. Gyeyke, "Aristotle on Language and Meaning," *International Philosophical Quarterly* 14 (1974): 71–77; Norman Kretzmann, "Aristotle on Spoken Sound Significant by Convention," in *Ancient Logic and Its Modern Interpretations*, edited by John Corcoran (Dordrecht, 1974), 3–21; and Eden, "Hermeneutics and the Ancient Rhetorical Tradition," 73–74.

11. On this judgment against obscurity and its subsequent history, see George L. Kustas, *Studies in Byzantine Rhetoric* (Thessaloniki, 1973), ch. 3, "The Concept of Obscurity in Greek Literature," 63–100.

Quintilian 7.9.15).[12] For quality considers which of two competing claims, such as *scriptum* and *voluntas*, is more just on a particular occasion (cf. Quintilian 7.7.2), whereas equity, as far back as its earliest formulation by Aristotle, not only associates itself with the intention of defendant and lawgiver alike, as we have seen, but also offers a necessary correction (Gr. *epanorthōma*) to the law's generality by taking account of the infinite variety and variability of human circumstance:

> Hence, while the equitable is just, and is superior to one sort of justice, it is not superior to absolute justice (*ou tou haplos*), but only to the error (*hamartēma*) due to its absolute statement (*dia to haplos*). This is the essential nature of the equitable: it is a rectification (*epanorthōma*) of law where law is defective because of its generality. In fact this is the reason why things are not all determined by law: it is because there are some cases for which it is impossible to lay down a law, so that a special ordinance becomes necessary. For what is itself indefinite can only be measured by an indefinite standard, like the leaden rule used by Lesbian builders; just as that rule is not rigid but can be bent to the shape of the stone, so a special ordinance is made to fit the circumstances of the case.
> [*Nicomachean Ethics* 5.10.6–7]

Equity, in other words, surpasses the law through its power to accommodate the individual case; and the equitable person, in turn, is one who does not enforce the law's stringency on his own behalf. He is not, in Aristotle's terms, *akribodikaios* (*Nicomachean Ethics* 5.10.8).[13]

12. On the status system, see Otto Alvin Loeb Dieter, "Stasis," *Speech Monographs* 17, no. 4 (1950): 345–69; Ray Nadeau, "Classical Systems of Stasis in Greek: Hermagoras to Hermogenes," *Greek, Roman and Byzantine Studies* 2, no. 1 (1959): 51–71, and "Hermogenes' *On Stases*: A Translation with an Introduction and Notes," *Speech Monographs* 31, no. 4 (1964): 361–424; and Wayne N. Thomson, "Stasis in Aristotle's *Rhetoric*," *Quarterly Journal of Speech* 58 (1972): 134–41. On the relation between the *status qualitatis* and equity, see Trimpi, *Muses of One Mind*, 245–75.

13. For an earlier opposition between *epeikōs* and *akribōs*, see Isocrates, *Helen*, 5 and n. 16 below. See also Eden, *Poetic and Legal Fiction in the Aristotelian Tradition*, 43–45.

Equity's accommodative power—that is, its responsiveness to particular circumstances—renders it a formidable tool of rhetorical argument, insofar as rhetoric itself is first and foremost the art of accommodation. Debating many other issues throughout the *De oratore*, Crassus and Antonius agree on this point (*De oratore* 1.31.138, 1.51.260). In its application to questions arising over written documents, equity is also, as part of the rhetorical tradition, a formidable tool of interpretation.[14]

So Cicero notes that the advocate of *voluntas* necessarily supports his case with a claim for equity. "For it would be the height of impudence," he contends, "for one who wishes to gain approval for some act *contra scriptum* not to gain his point with the help of equity (*aequitas*)" (*De inventione* 2.46.136, cf. 2.47.138); and Lucius Crassus's recollection in the *De oratore* of his victory in the so-called *causa curiana* confirms this contention.

Named for the plaintiff, Manius Curius, the famous *causa curiana* concerns a stipulation in the will of someone named Coponius that if a son were born to him and that son should die before being able to inherit, then Manius Curius should be heir. Soon thereafter Coponius dies childless; his next of kin, Marcus Coponius, claims the inheritance. So does Manius Curius. Quintus Scaevola, Crassus's adversary in court, upholds the *scriptum* of Coponius's will, arguing that since no son was born, Manius Curius has no claim. On the plaintiff's behalf, Crassus argues to uphold not only the testator's intention—that Manius Curius be second in line to inherit—but also equity (*De oratore* 1.39.180, 1.57.242, 2.32.140–41; cf. Quintilian 7.6.7–11).[15]

Without mentioning the *causa curiana* by name, the earlier *De inventione* nevertheless invokes it to illustrate one of the two kinds of claims made by advocates of *voluntas*. In one class of cases, Cicero advises, "[The] one who bases his defence on the intent will . . . show that the intent of the writer always had the same end in view and desired the same result" (*De inventione* 2.42.122), continuing, by way of example, with this well-known

---

14. In later chapters I explore the extent to which interpretation, like rhetorical composition, involves accommodation. For the hermeneutical potential of Aristotelian equity, see Hans-Georg Gadamer, *Truth and Method*, translated by Joel Weinsheimer and Donald G. Marshall (New York, 1989), 318–24.

15. For a case in which Crassus upholds the letter of the law against Antonius's plea for equity, see Cicero *De officiis* 3.16.67.

hypothesis: "A head of a family, having a wife but no children, drew his will as follows: 'If one or more sons are born to me, he or they are to inherit my estate.' Then comes, 'If my son dies before coming of age, then So-and-So is to be my heir.' No son was born. The agnates dispute with the man who was to be the reversionary heir in case the son died before coming of age" (2.42.122–23).

In a second class of cases, however, the advocate of *voluntas* argues rather that the writer's intention is not absolute (*simplex*) but must be interpreted to accommodate the particular occasion (*tum ex facto aut ex eventu aliquo ad tempus id quod instituit accommodabitur*) (*De inventione* 2.42.122). In these cases, Cicero continues, the argument gains support from its alliance with equity:

> But there is another kind of argument brought forward by advocates of the intent in which the wish of the writer is shown not to be absolute (*simplex*), *i.e.*, having the same weight for every occasion and for every action, but it is argued that his wishes ought to be interpreted (*interpretanda*) to fit the occasion in the light of some act or some event. This argument will be supported largely by topics under the assumptive branch of the issue of equity. (2.42.123)

The interpretive tradition that Cicero inherits as part of the rhetorical tradition, in other words, follows Aristotle not only in aligning equity with intentionality but also in recognizing the limitations of any written statement, whether in the form of a law or a will, to take account of each and every eventuality or set of circumstances that may come under its sway. In characterizing the indispensable function of equity as a corrective to the law, Aristotle rectifies this limitation with the fiction of the resurrected lawmaker:

> When therefore the law lays down a general rule, and thereafter a case arises which is an exception to the rule, it is then right, where the lawgiver's pronouncement because of its absoluteness (*haplos*) is defective and erroneous, to rectify (*epanorthoun*) the defect by

deciding as the lawgiver would himself decide if he
were present on the occasion, and would have
enacted if he had been cognizant of the case in question. [*Nicomachean Ethics* 5.10.5–6]

Echoing here Aristotle's specialized terminology (that is, Gr. *haploos*, Lat. *simplex*), Cicero appropriates his predecessor's insight in full, even as far as the resurrected lawmaker.[16] Rehearsing the strategies for arguing *contra scriptum*, he advises the advocate to claim "that the author of the law him-self, if he should rise from the dead, would approve this act, and would have done the same if he had been in a similar situation" (*De inventione* 2.47.139). Indeed, so fundamental is the need in legal interpretation for accommodating unspecified or unforeseen circumstances that Quintilian reinstates a ground of controversy discarded by Cicero's later works specifi-cally to facilitate just such an accommodation.

Reinstating, as it were, Cicero's *ratiocinatio,* yet without obscuring the substitution of terms (7.8.3; cf. 3.6.43), Quintilian's ground of controversy called *syllogismus* closely resembles the first ground of controversy, namely *scriptum/voluntas,* and not least of all in its reliance on equity (7.8.7). There is, however, one crucial difference. Whereas the advocate of *volun-tas,* properly speaking, argues *contra scriptum,* against the strict construc-tion of the law, the advocate of the *syllogistic basis* argues *supra scriptum,* beyond the strict construction of the law. And whereas the opponent of *voluntas* labors to secure "that in any case the letter may be carried into effect," the opponent of *syllogismus* aims to prevent "anything except the letter being carried into effect" (7.8.1). Or, as Quintilian explains else-where, "In investigations as to the *letter* and the *intention,* the dispute turns on the provisions contained in the law, whereas the *syllogism* deals with that which is not contained in the law" (7.10.3).

16. For the important history of *haploos* as a term in ethical and legal analysis, including its opposition to two other terms, *akribos* and *poikilos,* see Trimpi, *Muses of One Mind,* 116–43, 235–40. That Cicero understands the legal formulation that is absolute or *simplex* in opposition to one that needs to be accommodated is clear at 2.42.123: "In this kind of case [i.e., where the intention is *simplex*] it cannot be said that the intent of the writer ought to be made to fit some time or some event (*ad tempus et ad eventum aliquem sententiam scriptoris oportere accommodari*), because the only possible meaning is shown to be that on which the lit-igant who opposes the literal interpretation (*contra scriptum*) of the will defends his own right to inherit."

Only seemingly over-subtle, Quintilian's distinction between *contra scriptum* and *supra scriptum* follows Aristotle in appreciating the inherent incapacity of any written document—legal or otherwise—to speak to all circumstances and, more precisely, to remain meaningful through time.[17] In league with the resurrected lawmaker, as we shall see in later chapters, this strategy of "rectifying" or "correcting" the written statement, transmitted as an integral part of *interpretatio scripti,* provides one of the two most widely used and highly regarded interpretive tools of this tradition. The other is context.

Not yet so called, context as a concept developed within *interpretatio scripti* actually represents two separate interpretive instruments: what we might call *historical* context, on one hand, and *textual* context, on the other.[18] Historical context includes all those particularities that routinely define the rhetorical occasion, such as time, place, persons, and so on—the *circumstantiae* of the later rhetorical and grammatical traditions.[19] For lack of better terminology, Quintilian, awkwardly citing Valgius's rendition of his teacher Apollodorus, calls it the *negotium,* translating the Greek *peristasis* (literally *circumstantia*), defined as a *congregatio,* or congregation of persons, times, places, causes, means, incidents, acts, instruments, and so on (3.5.17–18).[20] These particularities, as we shall see later, constitute equally the grounds of decorum, the single most important principle of

17. Indeed, Quintilian follows Cicero in broadening this category to include not only anything written but also anything spoken (e.g., *De inventione* 2.47.140; *De oratore* 1.57.243; Quintilian 3.3.2).

18. I consider the development of this specialized term, including its early association with weaving, in later chapters. But see Quintilian 10.7.13.

19. On the *circumstantiae,* see Rita Copeland, *Rhetoric, Hermeneutics and Translation in the Middle Ages* (Cambridge, 1991), 63–86; R. W. Hunt, "The Introduction to the 'Artes' in the Twelfth Century," in *The History of Grammar in the Middle Ages,* edited by G. L. Bursill-Hall (Amsterdam, 1980), 117–44, esp. 125–26; A. J. Minnis, *Medieval Theory of Authorship,* 2d ed. (Philadelphia, 1988), 16–17; Martin Irvine, *The Making of Textual Culture: 'Grammatica' and Literary Theory, 350–1100* (Cambridge, 1994), 121–26; Edwin A. Quain, "The Medieval Accessus ad Auctores," *Traditio* 3 (1945): 215–64; and D. W. Robertson, Jr., "A Note on the Classical Origin of 'Circumstances' in the Medieval Confessional," *Studies in Philology* 43 (1946): 6–14.

20. See also Quintilian 5.10.20–52, where he lists the circumstances as pertaining either to *persons* (*personae*) or to *things* (*res*) and divides things into *causa, tempus, locus, occasio, instrumentum,* and *modus.*

In his *De rhetorica,* ch. 7, Augustine translates *peristaseis* as *circumstantiae,* defined as a

composition; and decorum, as we shall also see, is the productive counterpart to the receptive or interpretive principle of historical context.

Textual context, on the other hand, includes not only those passages that precede and follow the questionable text, but also the entire work from which it comes. So, Cicero advises the advocate in training:

> [I]t must be shown that from what precedes or follows the document (*ex superiore et ex inferiore scriptura*) the doubtful point becomes plain. Therefore, if words are to be considered separately by themselves, every word, or at least many words, would seem ambiguous (*ambigua*); but it is not right to regard as ambiguous what becomes plain on consideration of the whole context (*ex omni considerata scriptura*). In the next place, one ought to estimate what the writer meant from his other writings (*ex scriptis*), acts (*factis*), words (*dictis*), disposition (*animo*) and in fact his whole life (*vita*), and to examine the whole document which contains the ambiguity in question in all its parts, to see if any thing is apposite to our interpretation or opposed to the sense in which our opponent understands it. For it is easy to estimate what it is likely that the writer intended from the complete context (*ex omni scriptura*) and from the character of the writer (*ex persona scriptoris*), and from the qualities which are associated with certain characters. [*De inventione* 2.40.117]

Cicero, in other words, fully appreciates and indeed institutes contextualization of both kinds as powerful tools of interpretation; in so doing, he also acknowledges a priority fundamental to much Greco-Roman philosophical thinking—namely, the priority of the whole over the part. The advocate in training is thus encouraged to consider both the *whole* text and the *whole* set of circumstances that inform its production.

---

congregatio of particulars including *quis, quid, quando, ubi, cur, quem ad modum*, and *quibus adminiculis*. See C. Halm, *Rhetores Latini Minores* (Leipzig, 1863; rpt. Dubuque, Iowa, n.d.). For more on Augustine, see below, 54–56.

In the rhetorical tradition, moreover, this elevation of the whole over the part is already aligned with intentionality and equity. For in the same widely acknowledged passage of the *Rhetoric* that upholds the legislator's intention above his words and the defendant's intention above his actions, Aristotle further characterizes equity as upholding the whole (*to holon*) over the part (*to meros*) (*Rhetoric* 1.13.18), including the quality of the defendant's whole life—what sort of person he is always or for the most part (*hōs epi to polu*), in contrast to now, at this particular moment (cf. *De oratore* 2.29.100). Cicero agrees with Aristotle, in other words, that what an agent meant to do or say is best understood in the broadest possible context.

Like the equitable judgment, then, the broadly contextualized interpretation reads the part within the whole and the word (or deed) in light of the intention of the *scriptor* (or *actor*). In the rhetorical tradition of *interpretatio scripti*, as subsequent chapters will confirm and Erasmus's "Letter to Dorp" has already suggested, advocates of controversial readings and theorists of interpretation often follow the advice of these ancient rhetorical manuals not only in aligning intentionality with wholeness but in seeking this wholeness in the context of the particularities of both history and the text itself.

CHAPTER TWO

Hermeneutics and Ancient Grammar

Enarratio poetarum

I n the course of his duties, as we have seen, the ancient orator routinely defended interpretations of controversial texts, such as laws, contracts, and wills. In preparation for this kind of advocacy, the rhetorical manuals not only categorized the grounds of controversy but also provided strategies for resolving them in one's favor. Before undergoing such rhetorical training, however, the same young orator would have completed his course of study with the grammarian insofar as grammar served in the curriculum as the customary propaedeutic for rhetoric.[1] As part of his grammatical training, moreover, the schoolboy confronted equally challenging texts, primarily those of the poets. Indeed interpreting poetry—Gr. *exēgēsis poiētōn,* Lat. *enarratio poetarum*—constituted the principal preoccupation of the grammarian and his students.[2]

1. On this matter, see, e.g., Dio Chrysostom 53.1; Quintilian 2.1.1–2.2.1; Suetonius *De grammaticis* 4; and, more recently, Stanley F. Bonner, *Education in Ancient Rome* (Berkeley, 1977), 41–75, 181–276; Robert A. Kaster, *Guardians of Language: The Grammarian and Society in Late Antiquity* (Berkeley, 1988), 15–95; and H.-I. Marrou, *A History of Education in Antiquity,* translated by George Lamb (New York, 1956), 160–75.

2. Quintilian divides the art into correct speaking, *recte loquendi scientia,* and interpretation of the poets, *enarratio poetarum* (1.4.2), including in the latter the four Varronian *officia* of reading (Lat. *lectio,* Gr. *anagnōsis*), correcting (Lat. *emendatio,* Gr. *diorthōsis*), explaining (Lat. *enarratio,* Gr. *exēgēsis*) and judging (Lat. *iudicium,* Gr. *krisis*) (1.4.3). For both the differences and similarities between this four-part division of *enarratio poetarum* and Dionysius Thrax's six-part division, see F. H. Colson, "The Grammatical Chapters in Quintilian 1.4–8," *Classical Quarterly* 8 (1914): 33–47. See also P. B. R. Forbes, "Greek Pioneers in Philology and Grammar," *Classical Review* 47 (1933): 105–12; Martin Irvine, *The Making of Textual Culture: 'Grammatica' and Literary Theory, 350–1100* (Cambridge, 1994), 1–55; and R. H. Robins, "Dionysius Thrax and the Western Grammatical Tradition," *Transactions of the Philological Society* (1957): 67–106. For Sextus Empiricus's slightly different division of the grammatical art, see *Adv. math.* 1.91–93.

Like the rhetoricians, then, the grammarians addressed the difficulties arising from textual obscurity; and like the rhetorical art, as we shall see, the grammatical art, in the interest of resolving these obscurities, taught many of the same hermeneutical strategies for resolving ambiguities and contradictions and for weighing the competing claims of what the poet said, his *verba* or *scriptum,* and what he meant, his *voluntas.* In fact, the two most powerful interpretive tools of the orator (especially the forensic orator)—namely, historical context and textual context—receive their fullest treatment as part of the grammatical tradition.

Although this overlapping between the rhetorical and grammatical arts is not altogether unexpected, given the complementarity of the two disciplines, the fundamentally adversarial nature of grammatical exegesis—indeed of all interpretation in this tradition—runs somewhat counter to expectation. And yet the oldest extant instance of literary exegesis is profoundly adversarial.

In the *Protagoras* (338E–348A), Plato has Socrates and the eponymous sophist engage in intellectual combat over the meaning of an ode by Simonides. After establishing that sound literary exegesis—the kingdom of the grammarian—epitomizes the virtues of a liberal education (339A), Protagoras challenges Socrates to resolve the apparent contradictions and ambiguities in Simonides' poem. For Simonides claims in one passage that "to become truly good is hard" (339B), while in another he refutes Pittacus's nearly identical statement that it is "[h]ard . . . to be good" (339C).[3]

Likening Protagoras's explication of the inconsistency and consequent formal deficiency of the Simonidean ode to the knockout punch of a skillful boxer (339E), Socrates, after a quick recovery, takes the offensive with an astonishing display of his own exegetical skill—astonishing not so

---

3. For this and all other references to the text, I have used Plato, *Protagoras,* translated by W. R. M. Lamb, Loeb Classical Library (London, 1924). For further treatment of this episode, see Kathy Eden, "Hermeneutics and the Ancient Rhetorical Tradition," *Rhetorica* 5 (1987): 62–69; Dorothea Frede, "The Impossibility of Perfection: Socrates' Criticism of Simonides' Poem in the *Protagoras,*" *Review of Metaphysics* 39 (1986): 729–53; Hermann Gundert, "Die Simonides-Interpretation in Platons Protagoras," in *EPMHNEIA: Festschrift Otto Regenbogen* (Heidelberg, 1952), 71–93; and Rudolf Pfeiffer, *History of Classical Scholarship from the Beginnings to the End of the Hellenistic Age* (Oxford, 1968), 32ff.

much for its actual resolution of the contradictions as for the strategies it deploys in this effort.[4]

Clearly anticipating both the later rhetorical tradition of interpretation outlined in the previous chapter and Aristotle's specialized terminology for defining equity in the *Ethics* (see above, 13–17), Socrates claims to be seeking a fair and just reading, an *epanorthōma*, of Simonides's poem, one that will sustain the judgment, or *gnōmē*, of others (340AB), without, in its effort at correction, introducing any greater error, or *hamartēma* (340D). To this end, Socrates, like the forensic orator, calls to witness (341E, *mega tekmērion*; 344A, *martyrei*; 344D, *martyreitai*) both historical and textual context, including the changing signification of key words (341AB), the *comparanda* of other contemporary or nearly contemporary poetic passages (344A), other passages from the same text (341E), and finally the general intention of the whole poem (344B). For, as Socrates affirms, "[A]ll that comes after corroborates (*martyrei*) this view of [Simonides's] meaning" (344A).

On one hand, then, the interpretation of any single passage, in Socrates' expressed view, must find confirmation in the interpretation of the entire poem—the part, in other words, depending on the whole. On the other hand, the aim of this and all interpretation, formulated in distinctly legal language, is an understanding of the writer's meaning or intention, his *dianoia* (341E; 347A).[5] In the case of this particular ode, Socrates argues, the poet, Simonides, intends to refute his opponent, Pittacus.

4. Although Pfeiffer in his *History of Classical Scholarship from the Beginnings to the End of the Hellenistic Age*, 37, 203, and 272, characterizes the art of grammar as a Hellenistic innovation, see N. J. Richardson, "Homeric Professors in the Age of the Sophists," *Proceedings of the Cambridge Philological Society* 21 (1975): 65–81, and "Aristotle's Reading of Homer and Its Background," in *Homer's Ancient Readers: The Hermeneutics of Greek Epic's Earliest Exegetes*, edited by Robert Lamberton and John J. Keaney (Princeton, 1992), 30–40; and G. L. Huxley, "Historical Criticism in Aristotle's *Homeric Questions*," *Proceedings of the Royal Irish Academy* 79 (1979): 73–81.

On Plato the *grammatikos*, especially in the *Phaedrus*, see Irvine, *The Making of Textual Culture*, 25–30.

5. In keeping with the art of rhetoric, the grammatical art divides meaning into intention and signification—what agents mean and what words mean. So Varro, for instance, distinguishes in the *De lingua latina* between the *voluntas* of the *impositor* and the *significationes* of his words (7.1.1; cf. 7.1.2), while Sextus discredits separately the claim of knowing semantic meaning or signification (*Adv. math.* 1.36–38) and that of knowing authorial intention, the

If not a compelling reading of Simonides' intention, refutation very clearly characterizes both Socrates' intention in this peculiar exegetical exercise and, indeed, the intention of much ancient literary interpretation after Plato. Preserving in a highly condensed format the more ample literary solutions of the *Homeric Problems*, chapter 25 of Aristotle's *Poetics*, reinforcing Plato's legal language, defends poetry against the charges (*epitimēmata*) of its detractors by recommending many of the same strategies that we have examined so far as part of the rhetorical tradition of interpretation.[6]

Like Socrates in the *Protagoras*, Aristotle begins by advocating a fair and just reading of the literary text, one which, resembling the equitable judgment of his *Rhetoric* and *Ethics*, looks to the literary intention, or *prohairēsis*, of the artist as agent (25, 1460b16–21). In contrast to this fair-minded critic, the ones described disapprovingly by Glaucon base their judgments against the poets not on carefully considered evidence from the text but on unexamined prejudice (25, 1461a35–1461b3). To be judged fairly, however, contradictions and ambiguities must be contextualized, historically and textually.

Without explicitly distinguishing the two kinds of context, Aristotle recommends in some cases broad knowledge of the customs and practices of other cultures, especially past cultures (25, 1461a1–4), and in other cases, the circumstances informing apparently unseemly statements or

---

aim of exegesis (1.320). Aulus Gellius records the opposition between Chrysippus and Diodorus in terms of this same division (*Noctes Atticae* 11.12.1–3): whereas Chrysippus argues that all words are ambiguous, that is, capable of multiple signification, Diodorus argues, on the contrary, that no word is ambiguous unless the speaker so intends it.

For the Stoic definition of ambiguity see Diogenes Laertius *Lives of Eminent Philosophers* 7.62; for the grammarian on this issue as an aspect of signification see Aulus Gellius 5.18, 6.7, 6.11, 8.14, 9.12, 13.17, 18.7, 20.10, 20.11. For the analogy between words and laws in that the *significationes* of both change over time, see Aulus Gellius 12.13.5. See also Michael Frede, *Essays in Ancient Philosophy* (Minneapolis, 1987), ch. 16, "Principles of Stoic Grammar," 301–37, and ch. 17, "The Origins of Traditional Grammar," 338–59.

6. See Eden, "Hermeneutics and the Ancient Rhetorical Tradition," 69–75, *The Poetics of Aristotle* translated by Stephen Halliwell, (Chapel Hill, 1987), 176–80; G. L. Huxley, "Historical Criticism in Aristotle's *Homeric Questions*," 76–81; Rudolf Pfeiffer, *The History of Classical Scholarship from the Beginnings to the End of the Hellenistic Age*, 69–79; Thomas G. Rosenmeyer, "Design and Execution in Aristotle, *Poetics* ch. XXV," *California Studies in Classical Antiquity*, 6 (1973): 231–52.

actions. "When asking whether someone has spoken or acted morally or otherwise," Aristotle advises, "one should look to see not just if the deed or utterance is good or evil, but also to the identity of the agent or speaker, to the person with whom he deals, and to the occasion, means and purpose of what is done (e.g. whether the aim is to effect a greater good, or prevent a greater evil)" (25, 1461a4–9).[7] And this attention to the particularities of the case, familiar not only to all rhetorical analysis but also to the equitable judgment, serves equally in the resolution of contradictions (25, 1461b15–18). Indeed, contradictions often arise because of ambiguity caused by the inherent capacity of words to signify more than one thing and in more than one way. Here again Aristotle recommends context as a remedy: "Whenever a word appears to entail a contradiction, one should consider how many meanings are possible (*posachōs an sēmē neie*) in the linguistic context (*en tōi eirēmenōi*)" (25, 1461a31–35).[8]

Introducing this summary treatment of literary exegesis, as we have seen, with an even briefer analysis of artistic intention, Aristotle then turns to some equally elliptical remarks about style or *lexis* (25, 1461a9–31), dividing the question of meaning, much as the later rhetorical manuals will do, between intentionality and signification. Furthermore, his discussion of signification, as an aspect of style, focuses on the multiple ways that words can signify or, in other words, on metaphorical statement. For the interpreter of poetry must understand the nature and function of metaphor as the most effective instrument of style (25, 1461a16–21; cf. 25, 1460b11–12).[9]

The workings of metaphor are so fundamental to both the composition and reception or interpretation of discourse, spoken as well as written, that Aristotle, ensuring its status in the rhetorical and grammatical traditions, treats it at length both in the *Poetics* (chs. 19–22) and in the *Rhetoric* (3.2.6–3.11.16). Produced by genius or natural talent rather than art (*Rhetoric* 3.2.8; *Poetics* 22.17), metaphor derives its analogical relations from the same skill that makes the dialectician or philosopher—namely,

7. *The Poetics of Aristotle*, translated by Halliwell, 62.

8. Ibid.

9. For Aristotle on style, see above, 11–12; for Aristotle on metaphor, see William J. Jordan, "Aristotle's Concept of Metaphor in Rhetoric," in *Aristotle: The Classical Heritage of Rhetoric*, edited by Keith V. Erickson (Metuchen, N.J., 1974), 235–50.

the ability to detect likeness and difference (*Poetics* 22.17; *Rhetoric* 2.20.7–8).
So Aristotle reminds the rhetorician in training that "metaphors should be
drawn from objects which are proper to the object (*apo oikeiōn*), but not
too obvious; just as, for instance, in philosophy it needs sagacity to grasp
the similarity in things that are apart" (3.11.5). Elsewhere he characterizes
this quality of being "proper," or *oikeios*—from the same *oikos* or house—
as being *sungenēs*—from the same *genos*, group or tribe.[10] While the
approved metaphor is at once *oikeia* and *sungenēs*, metaphors fail when
they are strange, unfamiliar, alien, or far-fetched—*allotriai* or *porrōthen:*
"Further, metaphors must not be far-fetched (*porrōthen*), but we must give
names to things that have none by deriving the metaphor from what is akin
(*ek tōn sungenōn*) and of the same kind, so that, as soon as it is uttered, it is
clearly seen to be akin (*sungenēs*)" (*Rhetoric* 3.2.12, cf. 3.3.4, 3.10.6; *Poetics*
21.15).

The most excellent metaphors, in other words, strike the listener sud-
denly, even unexpectedly (cf. *Rhetoric* 3.11.6), as *oikeiai* or *sungeneis*, as
belonging to the matter at hand. Like the most approved tragedies of the
Poetics, especially *Oedipus the King* and *Iphigenia in Tauris*, these metaphors uncover some profound relationship, some unforeseen familiarity
between two seemingly unrelated entities.[11] Aristotle also qualifies them as
prepeis and *epieikeis* (see 3.2.9–10, 3.2.12–13, and 3.3.4). Not only indi-

10. Both *genos* and *oikeios*, as terms that shape Plato's conception of dialectic—the
process, according to Aristotle, fundamental to metaphorical thinking—belong originally to
the domestic arena. The language of logical relation, in other words, reflects its origin in family relation. See, e.g., *Statesman*, translated by Harold N. Fowler, Loeb Classical Library
(London, 1925), 25AB: "when a person at first sees only the unity or common quality
(*koinōnian*) of many things, he must not give up until he sees all the differences in them, so
far as they exist in classes; and conversely, when all sorts of dissimilarities are seen in a large
number of objects he must find it impossible to be discouraged or to stop until he has gath-
ered into one circle of similarity all the things which are related to each other (*ta oikeia*) and
has included them in some sort of class (*genous*) on the basis of their essential nature." For
Aristotle's use of *oikeion* and its derivatives in the *Poetics* (1453a29, 1455b13, and 1459b28),
see Roos Meijering, *Literary and Rhetorical Theories in Greek Scholia* (Groningen, 1987),
150–52, 164–71. For the opposition between *oikeia* and *allotria* in Pindar, see A. M. Miller,
"*Inventa componere*: Rhetorical Process and Poetic Composition in Pindar's Ninth Olympian
Ode," *Transactions of the American Philological Association* 123 (1993): 109–47, esp. 116.

11. For further analogies between tragic representation and metaphor in Aristotle's
thinking see Kathy Eden, *Poetic and Legal Fiction in the Aristotelian Tradition* (Princeton,
1986), 71.

vidually but in relation to one another, each of these terms—*prepēs, epieikēs, oikeia*—figures prominently in the tradition of interpretation we are tracing.[12]

As we have seen, equity—Gr. *epieikeia*—corrects the rigidity and generality of the law by accommodating the particular circumstances of the case. In matters of style, this accommodative function is served by the principle called *to prepon* by Aristotle (*Rhetoric* 3.7.1–11) and the subsequent Greek tradition and *decorum* by the Latin tradition, including Cicero and Quintilian.[13] Indeed, Cicero defines eloquence as the ability to practice *decorum*, defined in turn as the ability to accommodate the occasion, taking account of times, places, and persons: "This, indeed, is the form of wisdom that the orator must especially employ—to adapt himself to occasions and persons. In my opinion one must not speak in the same style at all times, nor before all people, nor against all opponents, nor in defence of all clients, nor in partnership with all advocates. He, therefore, will be eloquent who can adapt his speech to fit all conceivable circumstances (*Is erit ergo eloquens, qui ad id quodcumque decebit poterit accommodare orationem*)" (*Orator* 123). Reminding us in the *Orator* of the pairing of terms in Greek and Latin (70–71), Cicero also reminds us that such accommodation makes or breaks one's efforts not only in oratory but also in poetry and even in life. As it affects poetry, he continues, *decorum* comes under the careful consideration of the *grammaticus* (*Orator* 72). For the interpretation of poetry, as the grammarian's chief function, depends in large part on the very same set of questions asked by the orator in the interests of *decorum:* who, to whom, when, where, why, and so on.

Later becoming the *circumstantiae* of the grammatical tradition, these questions combine to provide the grammarian with one of his most powerful interpretive tools—historical context. In his most influential discussion of grammar in the first book of the *Institutio Oratoria*, Quintilian does

12. Throughout his treatment of style, Aristotle establishes the closest relation between *to prepon* and *to oikeion*, at times insisting on little or no distinction between them. See, e.g., 3.7.4 and 3.7.7.
13. See Wesley Trimpi, "Horace's 'Ut Pictura Poesis': The Argument for Stylistic Decorum," *Traditio* 34 (1978): 29–73, *Muses of One Mind: The Literary Analysis of Experience and Its Continuity* (Princeton, 1983), esp. 83–240, and "Reason and the Classical Premises of Literary Decorum," *Independent Journal of Philosophy* 5/6 (1988): 103–11.

not explicitly draw the parallels between *decorum* as an instrument of rhetorical composition and historical context as an instrument of literary interpretation or reception.[14] He does, however, both single out *decorum* as one of the two concepts indispensable to the young student at the start of his exegetical training (1.8.17) and identify literary exegesis—elsewhere called *enarratio poetarum*—with the branch of grammar characterized as *historice* (1.9.1, cf. 1.4.2 and 1.8.18–21).[15] Interpreting poetry, in other words, is fundamentally a historical investigation, one grounded in the very questions that constitute the principle of *decorum*.

The other concept deemed indispensable to the young interpreter is *oeconomia* (Gr. *oikonomia*). A term with no Latin equivalent, according to Quintilian, it was borrowed from the domestic arena (*ex cura rerum domesticarum*) by the Greek Hellenistic rhetorician Hermagoras to cover the various elements of *elocutio*, or style (3.3.9).[16] Roman rhetoricians, however, seem to have applied it more exclusively to matters of arrangement, or *dispositio* (Gr. *taxis*), the second of the five rhetorical *partes*. Indeed, the role of *oeconomia* in disposition or arrangement corresponds to that of *decorum*

14. On the *circumstantiae*, see above, 17–18.

15. On the historical part of the grammatical art, as contrasted with the technical, called *methodice* by Quintilian, see also Varro 8.2.6 and Sextus Empiricus *Adv. math.* 1.92–93. According to Suetonius *De grammaticis* 10, the art of history-writing has two comparable parts, the historical (*breviarium rerum omnium Romanarum*) and the technical (*ratio scribendi*).

For the role of history in the grammarian's art, see *De oratore* 1.187, and for its relation to rhetoric, see Gerald A. Press, *The Development of the Idea of History in Antiquity* (Montreal, 1982), and Nancy Struever, *The Language of History in the Renaissance* (Princeton, 1970), esp. 1–37. That rhetoric and historiography should be complementary arts in antiquity is not surprising given their common stake in contingency and particularity.

16. So Cicero, writing to his brother, Atticus, leaves the Greek *oikonomia* not only untranslated but even untransliterated (*Letters to Atticus*, vol. 1, translated by E. O. Winstedt, Loeb Classical Library [London, 1919], 415: "nor will I start an arrangement of my own, but will keep to your order (*nec οἰκονομίαν meam instituam, sed ordinem conservabo tuum*)." On the role of *oeconomia* in ancient exegesis, see David Dawson, *Allegorical Readers and Cultural Revision in Ancient Alexandria* (Berkeley, 1992), esp. 58–77; Malcolm Heath, *Unity in Greek Poetics* (Oxford, 1989); Roos Meijering, *Literary and Rhetorical Theories in Greek Scholia*, esp. 134–225; and N. J. Richardson, "Literary Criticism in the Exegetical Scholia to the *Iliad*: A Sketch," *Classical Quarterly* 30 (1980): 265–87.

See also my "Economy in the Hermeneutics of Late Antiquity," in *Reconfiguring the Relation Rhetoric/Hermeneutics*, edited by George Pullman, *Studies in the Literary Imagination* 28 (1995): 13–26.

(Gr. *to prepon*) in elocution or style, in that it serves to accommodate the particular case.

Whereas *taxis* or *dispositio* refers to a straightforward organization of the material, one that follows both the natural order of events and the conventional order of composition, *oeconomia* follows a more indirect, artificial organization, one altered specifically to accommodate the circumstances of the case, with the special end of arousing the audience's emotions. Both the author of the *Ad Herennium* (3.16–17) and Cicero (*De oratore* 2.76.307) discuss this more devious kind of arrangement, while the *Ad Herennium* actually refers to it as an accommodation: *oratoris iudicio ad tempus accommodatur* (3.17, cf. 3.16: *ad casum temporis accommodatum*).[17]

Like *decorum* in its commitment to the particularities of the case, *oeconomia* is also like *decorum* in subordinating the rules of art to the play of natural talent:

> For the most effective, and what is justly styled most
> *economical* arrangement (*oeconomica dispositio*) of a case
> as a whole, is that which cannot be determined except
> when we have the specific facts before us. It consists in
> the power to determine when the *exordium* is neces-
> sary and when it should be omitted; when we should
> make our statement of facts continuous, and when we
> should subdivide it; when we should begin at the very
> beginning, when, like Homer (*more Homerico*), start at
> the middle or the end. [Quintilian 7.10.11–12]

As Quintilian suggests, this oratorical *economy* closely resembles the most excellent poetic composition, the *mos Homericus*, characterized earlier by the well-known Horatian phrase *in medias res* (*Ars Poetica* 148).[18] As prac-

---

17. See Meijering, *Literary and Rhetorical Theories in Greek Scholia*, 141–43, and J. Reumann, "οἰκονομία as 'Ethical Accommodation' in the Fathers, and Its Pagan Background," *Studia Patristica* 3 (1961): 370–79. See also Marvin T. Herrick, *Comic Theory in the Sixteenth Century*, Illinois Studies in Language and Literature 34 (1950): 98–106. Cf. Longinus, 1.4, where *taxis* and *oikonomia* are said to emerge from the work as a whole.

18. Irvine, *The Making of Textual Culture*, 131, quotes Servius's Preface to his Commentary on the *Aeneid*: "The order of the books is also obvious, although some say unnecessarily that the second is first, the third second, and the first third, since Ilium falls first, and then Aeneas wanders, arriving at queen Dido's land; they are ignorant, therefore, that this is

ticed by orators as well as poets, this kind of composition takes as its starting point a decisive relation between the whole and its parts. Indeed, it presupposes the whole in composing the parts.[19]

To discuss this special coherence of discourse as a unified multiplicity, Quintilian relies not only on the traditional metaphor of organic unity but, more important for our purposes, on that of the social unit, or *societas*, in which no member suffers estrangement but all are familiar, at home.[20] So organized, Quintilian claims, discourse, or *oratio*, is not merely arranged in its parts (*composita*) but whole and complete (*continua*):

> And it is not enough merely to arrange the various parts: each several part has its own internal economy, according to which one thought will come first, another second, another third, while we must struggle not merely to place these thoughts in their proper order, but to link them together and give them such cohesion that there will be no trace of any suture: they must form a body, not a congeries of limbs (*corpus sit,*

---

poetical art, so that beginning in the middle of things by the narration we return to first things and sometimes anticipate things about to happen, as if by prophecy. Horace also gives a precept in the *Ars Poetica* as follows: 'So that [the poet] says now what ought to be said just now, and postpones or omits many things for the time being (*Ars Poet.* 43–4).' It follows that Virgil has done this expertly."

19. Although the discovery of this relation is often misattributed to the philosophical hermeneutics of the past century, it goes back, as some have recognized, to antiquity. See especially Hans-Georg Gadamer, *Truth and Method*, translated by Joel Weinsheimer and Donald Marshall (New York, 1989), 175–78, esp. 291–300: "We recall the hermeneutical rule that we must understand the whole in terms of the detail and the detail in terms of the whole. This principle stems from ancient rhetoric, and modern hermeneutics has transferred it to the art of understanding. It is a circular relationship in both cases. The anticipation of meaning in which the whole is envisaged becomes actual understanding when the parts that are determined by the whole themselves also determine this whole. . . . Thus the movement of understanding is constantly from the whole to the part and back to the whole. Our task is to expand the unity of the understood meaning centrifugally. The harmony of all the details with the whole is the criterion of correct understanding. The failure to achieve this harmony means that understanding has failed" (192). See also Leo Spitzer, *Linguistics and Literary Theory* (Princeton, 1948), 19–29, esp. nn. 9–10, and David Couzens Hoy, *The Critical Circle: Literature, History, and Philosophical Hermeneutics* (Berkeley, 1978).

20. Both the organic metaphor and the "political" go back to Plato. See, e.g., *Phaedrus* 264C, 268D; *Gorgias* 507E–508A; and *Statesman* 285AB.

non membra). This end will be attained if we note
what best suits each position, and take care that the
words which we place together are such as will not
clash, but will mutually harmonise (*complectantur*).
Thus different facts will not seem like perfect
strangers (*ignotae*) thrust into uncongenial company
from distant places (*distantibus locis*), but will be
united with what precedes and follows by an intimate
bond of union (*societate*), with the result that our
speech will give the impression not merely of having
been put together (*composita*), but of natural continuity (*continua*). [7.10.16–17, cf. 10.7.14]

Borrowed from the domestic arena, as Quintilian has already reminded us,
and related to the *oikeia* of Aristotle's best metaphors, *oeconomia* (Gr.
oikonomia), in other words, takes social organization, based on the unit of
the family, the *oikos* (Lat. *domus*), as the shaping analogy for literary composition. Trained to applaud such unity in the literary work, Quintilian's
grammarian is also trained to recognize and sometimes even correct its
absence. In keeping with the metaphor at the root of *oeconomia*, he searches
out and on occasion rejects spurious lines as one would "[expell] a sup-
posititious child from the family circle" (1.4.3).

As literary interpreters and critics, then, grammarians in Quintilian's
day expect economy in the best forms of discourse. A formal property, literary economy works, like its counterpart, *decorum*, to accommodate the
particular occasion. Subordinating the individual parts of the discourse to
the overall plan of the whole, *oeconomia*, a principle of composition and
interpretation, presupposes the whole in the disposition of the parts. For
the interpreter, this presupposition justifies the concept of *textual context*,
further enforcing the alliance between *oeconomia* and *decorum*, which, as
we have seen, underlies the concept of *historical context*.

As an accommodation that grants priority to the whole over the parts,
oeconomia also corresponds as a formal principle to equity as an ethical
principle. Indeed, in the tradition we are tracing, the formal properties of
discourse are routinely understood in terms borrowed not only from the
ethical but even from the domestic arena, including the unit of the family

as well as that of the polity. This correspondence between formal and ethical categories, clearly reflected in Quintilian's analogy between economical arrangement (*oeconomica dispositio*) and a social unit, or *societas*, informs one especially influential work in the grammatical tradition—namely, Plutarch's essay on how the young should read poetry, the so-called *De audiendis poetis* (*Moralia* 14D–37B). For Plutarch, as I hope to show, understands the literary interpretive process itself as an *accommodation* in the radical sense of the term: as a coming to feel at home with the literary text, a process of making it familiar.[21]

As contemporary students of Plutarch regularly note, his instructions to the young reader, grounded in a mix of Platonic and Aristotelian presuppositions, advance an ethical reading of the poets, especially Homer.[22] These same students, however, frequently overlook the extent to which Plutarch inherits this method of reading from the same grammatical tradition outlined in the first book of Quintilian's *Institutio* (1.4.1–5), where the part of grammar called *enarratio poetarum*—the interpretation of poets—includes the four activities of reading, correcting, explicating, and judging literary texts (see above, 20n2).

Boldly subordinating formal to ethical concerns, Plutarch places the correction of texts, the second activity, in the service of the correction of

---

21. At *De natura deorum* 1.41, Cicero translates the Greek *sunoikeioun*, already a technical term of Stoic hermeneutics, as *accommodare*. See on this matter *M. Tulli Ciceronis de natura deorum*, vol. 1, edited by Arthur Stanley Pease (New York, 1979), 276. I am grateful to Dirk Obbink for this reference. See also A. A. Long, "Stoic Readings of Homer," in *Homer's Ancient Readers*, edited by Lamberton and Keaney, 41–66.

For the relation between *commodus* and *accommodare*, see *Ad Herennium*, 4.12.17: "Since I have discussed the types to which style should confine itself, let us now see what qualities should characterize an appropriate (*commoda*) and finished style. To be in fullest measure suitable (*adcommodata*) to the speaker's purpose such a style should have three qualities: Taste, Artistic Composition, and Distinction." The relation between *accommodating* and *making to feel at home* is preserved in the way a contemporary Italian still welcomes me into her home with "Stia comoda" or "Si accommodi."

I pursue further the relation between interpretation and accommodation in later chapters. Contemporary psychology and literary theory have continued to explore this relation without attention to its history. See, e.g., Jean Piaget, *The Construction of Reality in the Child*, translated by Margaret Cook (New York, 1954), esp. 395ff., and Tzvetan Todorov, *Symbolism and Interpretation*, translated by Catherine Porter (Ithaca, 1982), 27–28.

22. See, e.g., D. A. Russell, *Plutarch* (London, 1973), 43–53, and *Criticism in Antiquity* (London, 1981), 63, 85.

young moral characters.[23] Indeed, his usual choice of a term for the second of the four activities, *epanorthōsis*, in place of the more customary *diorthōsis* noted above, recalls not only Aristotle's formulation of equity as a correction or *epanorthōma* of the law but also Socrates' professed exegetical aim in the *Protagoras* (cf. *Moralia* 22B, 24B, 29D, 33D, 34B). Yet Plutarch follows the more traditional grammarians (and rhetoricians) in seeking to resolve ambiguities (e.g., 22CF, 24AF) and contradictions (e.g., 20CD), especially those caused by the inherent capacity of language to signify in more than one way. For the young reader, he advises, must learn "to adapt (*sunoikeioun*) the usage of the words to fit the matter in hand, as the grammarians teach us to do, taking a word for one signification at one time, and at another time for another" (22F).[24] Only by so doing can the interpreter reconcile the discrepancies between the author's words and intentions.

As soon as Plutarch's student begins to read poetry, in fact, he must be armed with the very same two principles of interpretation singled out by Quintilian as worthy of mention at the start of the grammarian's lesson: *decorum* and *oeconomia*, or in Plutarch's—and Aristotle's—Greek, *to prepon* and *to oikeion.*[25] Otherwise, the young reader may misinterpret the poet's intention in those passages representing deformity, by misunderstanding the relation between ethical and formal considerations:

> For by its essential nature the ugly cannot become
> beautiful; but the imitation, be it concerned with what
> is base or with what is good, if only it attain to the like-
> ness, is commended. If, on the other hand, it produces
> a beautiful picture of an ugly body, it fails to give
> what propriety (*to prepon*) and probability (*to eikos*)

---

23. For a comparison between Philodemus and Plutarch on reading poetry, especially as regards their subordination of grammar to philosophy, see Elizabeth Asmis, "Philodemus's Poetic Theory and *On the Good King According to Homer,*" *Classical Antiquity* 10 (1991): 1–45, esp. 21–22.

24. On *sunoikeioun* as a technical term of Stoic hermeneutics, see above, 31, and cf. Quintilian 1.8.11–46.

25. In this essay Plutarch does not use the term *oikonomia* as a technical term of exegesis perhaps because of its close association with Stoic metaphysics that he elsewhere rejects. See, e.g., *De stoicorum repugnantiis*, translated by Harold Cherniss, Loeb Classical Library (London, 1976), 13, 2, 1050AE, where the term in a metaphysical context still characterizes the relation of the parts to the whole.

require. . . . For it is not the same thing at all to imitate something beautiful and something beautifully,
since "beautifully" means "fittingly and properly"
(*prepontōs kai oikeiōs*) and ugly things are "fitting and
proper" (*oikeia de kai preponta*) for the ugly.[26] [18AD]

So, for instance, the reader should interpret Ixion's words not in isolation,
as discrete passages, but, recalling Cicero's advice to the young orator in
the *De inventione*, in the whole context of Ixion's character, his actions,
and, indeed, his whole life story; for it is fitting and proper that an ignoble
character speak ignobly and, as Euripides himself argues in his own
defense of this representation, end his life ignobly in the course of the
whole or completed drama (19E).[27]

Similarly, Plutarch argues, Aristarchus failed to contextualize and so
wrongly athetized Phoenix's narration in the *Iliad* of his murderous intentions toward his father. For this shocking tale of the effects of action moti-
vated by anger thoroughly suits the occasion (*pros ton kairon*)—Phoenix's
part in the embassy to Achilles in book 9. Its literary intention is confirmed,
moreover, by the passage that follows, Phoenix's story of Meleager
(26F–27A). Indeed, throughout this essay textual context (*ta parakeimena,
ta sumphrazomena*) provides the principal instrument of correction (e.g.,
22B).

While Plutarch's arguments look back ultimately to the Aristotelian
defense of fiction in the *Poetics*, especially chapters 4 and 25 (cf. *Rhetoric*
1.11.23–24, and see *Republic* 420CD), the interpretive strategies there
advanced by Aristotle had become part of the grammatical tradition long
before Plutarch's time.[28] In their efforts to accommodate—in the sense of
make familiar—unfamiliar texts, the earliest grammarians both practiced

26. For an English translation I have used throughout Plutarch, *Moralia*, vol. 1, translated
by Frank Cole Babbitt, Loeb Classical Library (London, 1927).

27. While Plutarch encourages the student to make the appropriate accommodations, he
roundly condemns the excessively accommodative nature (26B): "But the man who admires
everything, and accommodates himself (*exoikeioumenos*) to everything, whose judgment,
because of his preconceived opinion, is enthralled by the heroic names, will, like those who
copy Plato's stoop or Aristotle's lisp, unwittingly become inclined to conform to much that is
base." For other compounds with *oikeion*, see 22F, 27B, and 36D.

28. On these strategies, including *oikonomia*, see most recently Dawson, *Allegorical Readers and Cultural Revision in Ancient Alexandria;* Heath, *Unity in Greek Poetics;* Meijering,

and preached the contextualizing of problematic passages. As we have seen, *decorum* and *oeconomia* institutionalize these efforts at accommodation, and their application to poetry by Plutarch is traditional, especially in light of Quintilian's remark that the *mos Homericus* is characteristically *economical*. As a Platonist, however, Plutarch's call for the application of *decorum* and *oeconomia* to the interpretation of fiction is especially apt insofar as he outspokenly considers fiction itself an accommodation.

Whereas in the traditional curriculum, as previously noted, the student advances from grammar to rhetoric, Plutarch's student begins with poetry as a propaedeutic to philosophy (15F; cf. 37B). Reworking Plato's myth of the cave,[29] Plutarch compares poetry to the soft rays (*malakai augai*) of reflected light that accustom the eye to gaze directly at the sun—here philosophy: "But when they hear the precepts of the philosophers, which go counter to such opinions, at first astonishment and confusion and amazement take hold of them, since they cannot accept or tolerate any such teaching, unless, just as if they were now to look upon the sun after having been in utter darkness, they have been made accustomed, in a reflected light, as it were, in which the dazzling rays of truth are softened by combining truth with fable, to face facts of this sort without being distressed, and not to try to get away from them" (36E). Through the analogy with optics so familiar to students of Plato, Plutarch characterizes poetry as an accommodation to the weakness inherent in human physiology and psychology—here the need for contrast, differentiation, and nuance: that is, for change. And poetry not only mitigates the pain that accompanies the harshness and unemotional sameness of the truth, but it fully exploits the pleasure that comes from variety. Whereas philosophy pursues the truth along a single path, without change or deviation, fiction travels around (*perixōrei*), as it were, taking the indirect route (16B).

So firm is Plutarch's identification of fiction with variety that when he follows Aristotle in elevating the plot over the other elements of poetry by

---

Literary and Rhetorical Theories in Greek Scholia; and James I. Porter, "Hermeneutic Lines and Circles: Aristarchus and Crates on the Exegesis of Homer," *Homer's Ancient Readers,* edited by Lamberton and Keaney, 67–114. See also D. M. Schenkeveld, "The Structure of Plutarch's *De audiendis poetis,*" *Mnemosyne* 35 (1982): 60–71.

29. For Plutarch's Platonism, see Russell, *Plutarch,* 63–83, and *Criticism in Antiquity,* 90–91.

appropriating the analogy in the *Poetics* (ch. 17) between poetry and painting, he nevertheless reverses the Aristotelian priority of line over color. Whereas Aristotle identifies the plot with line, Plutarch identifies it with what is for him the more important element in painting, color, which provides the variegation so fundamental to the pleasure and thus the power of the mimetic arts (16BC). Further in keeping with this understanding, Plutarch likens the plot or narrative to a woven tapestry, whose color and complexity is aptly characterized as *poikilos*, like *poikilma*, or embroidery (16B, 25D).[30]

While the comparison between weaving and fictional discourse figures throughout Greek poetry, beginning with Homer,[31] Plutarch uses it in this essay not only to characterize his reading of Homer as the archetypal weaver of tales but, more particularly, to characterize his interpretation of the *Odyssey* as the archetypal tale about weaving tales. For Plutarch's conception of fiction resembles Homer's hero in that it reaches home (*oikos*)— in a sense, achieves familiarity as a fitting part of the community—not by

---

30. On *poikilia* as a literary term, see Trimpi, *Muses of One Mind*, 133–43, 235–40; Meijering, *Literary and Rhetorical Theories in Greek Scholia*, 168–71; Heath, *Unity in Greek Poetics*, 102–23; Richardson, "Literary Criticism in the Exegetical Scholia to the *Iliad*," 265–87; and David Young, "Pindar, Aristotle and Homer: A Study in Ancient Criticism," *Classical Antiquity* 2 (1983): 153–40. For the continued association of weaving and fiction in the Latin tradition, consider such terms as *textus, contextus,* and *integumentum.* On the last, see Peter Dronke, *Fabula: Explorations into the Uses of Myth in Medieval Platonism* (Leiden, 1974), esp. 48–52, 119–22.

A passage from the essay "Isis and Osiris" comments provocatively on Plutarch's position: "That these accounts do not, in the least, resemble the sort of loose fictions and frivolous fabrications which poets and writers of prose evolve from themselves, after the manner of spiders, interweaving (*huphainousi*) and extending their unestablished first thoughts, but that these contain narrations of certain puzzling events and experiences, you will yourself understand. Just as the rainbow, according to the account of the mathematicians, is a reflection (*emphasin*) of the sun, and owes its many hues (*poikillomenēn*) to the withdrawal of our gaze from the sun and our fixing it on the cloud, so the somewhat fanciful accounts here set down are but reflections (*emphasis*) of some true tale (*logou*) which turns back our thoughts to other matters" (*Moralia* 358F–359A). In the first part of this passage, fiction is compared to the spider's web, recalling the traditional analogy between discourse, especially poetic discourse, and weaving, while in the second, it is compared to the rainbow, which, through its variegated colors (*poikilia*), as a product of reflected as opposed to direct light, better accommodates our vision.

31. See, e.g., Jane McIntosh Snyder, "The Web of Song: Weaving Imagery in Homer and the Lyric Poets," *Classical Journal* 76 (1980–81): 193–96.

the direct route but, as it were, by traveling around; and like Plutarch's fiction, Odysseus's travels thematize the power of accommodation to effect the journey home. For Plutarch, in other words, the *mos Homericus*—Homer's way—is at once formal and ethical. Like other grammarians, Plutarch relies on the force of *oikonomia* as an interpretive strategy to preserve the integrity of the text. Like the philosopher, however, he also works to ensure the integrity of the young reader by enforcing the longstanding correspondence between the formal and ethical, particularly domestic, aspects of the conception of the *oikos* itself.

While rejecting the allegorical reading of Homer after the Stoic fashion (19F, cf. 31E), then, Plutarch may be practicing a more subtle allegorical reading of his own. Without by any means advocating a full-scale allegorical interpretation of Homer, Plutarch, I would like to speculate, advances his own arguments for the right way to read through an accommodation of Homer's story—that is, by reading parts of the *Odyssey* as an allegory of reading.[32]

Broadly speaking, Odysseus's landing on the shores of Ithaca signals the return from the dangers of alien culture—the physical and psychological alienation of the stranger—to the comfort of familiarity, of belonging to the *oikos*.[33] Of course, Odysseus enters the *oikos* as a stranger who must resume by trial his part in the community. In this as in his earlier trials, his success lay in his ability to accommodate the circumstances.

32. On the essay "Isis and Osiris" as an allegory of allegorical reading, see Dawson, *Allegorical Readers and Cultural Revision in Ancient Alexandria*, 60–61. On philosophical reading of Homer in late antiquity see Robert Lamberton, *Homer the Theologian: Neoplatonic Allegorical Reading and the Growth of the Epic Tradition* (Berkeley, 1986).

Probably a near-contemporary of Plutarch, 'Heraclitus' in his *Homeric Questions* evaluates the place of Homeric poetry in the life of the educated man of the first century: "From the earliest stage of life, our infant children in their first moments of learning are suckled on him; we are wrapped in his poems, one might also say, as babies, and nourish our minds on their milk. As the child grows and comes to manhood Homer is at his side, Homer shares his mature years, and the man is never weary of him even in old age. When we leave him, we feel the thirst again. The end of Homer is the end of life for us" (translated by Russell in *Criticism in Antiquity*, 191).

33. In *Truth and Method*, Gadamer locates hermeneutical activity between the poles of familiarity and estrangement: "Hermeneutic work is based on a polarity of familiarity and strangeness. . . . It is in the play between the traditionary text's strangeness and familiarity to us, between being a historically intended, distanciated object and belonging to the tradition. *The true locus of hermeneutics is this in-between*" (295). Also illuminating in light of the

Throughout Homer's poem the hero is thus characterized as *polumētis* and *polutropos*. And his accommodative nature finds its match in his domestic partner, Penelope, whose stratagem of the weaving thematizes not only the colorful web of words that accompanies her own handiwork but also the verbal weavings of both her husband and the poet (see *Odyssey* 2.93–109; 19.136–56). So when Plutarch characterizes fiction at 25D with the pair of terms *poikilos* and *polutropos*, he may be not only borrowing in particular from the scholiastic tradition of the *Odyssey* but also inviting the young reader more specifically to imagine the famous fictional pair, whose colorful tale of domestic reunion foregrounds these very qualities.[34]

Furthermore, because the special danger of reading is to be misled, the student must be cautioned against falsehood. Both Odysseus and Penelope complement their skill at telling tales with their reserve in believing the

---

traditionary status of the *Odyssey* and its role in this essay is Gadamer's reflection on the Greek term *oikos* in "*Logos* and *Ergon* in Plato's *Lysis*," in *Dialogue and Dialectic:* "As a matter of fact Socrates finds a word to express the character of this tension-laden relationship in which need and fulfillment coexist. It is the Greek word *oikeion*, i.e., that which pertains to the household, to the *oikos*. It is an ordinary expression for relatives and house friends, i.e., for all who belong to the household. Oikos, household, thus has the broad sense of an economic unity such as the Greek household characteristically was. But oikeion is just as much an expression for that place where one feels at home, where one belongs and where everything is familiar. . . . Socrates uses *oikeion* [in the *Lysis*] and its semantic field to say that there is a need in me of *das Zugehoerige*, a need of that which pertains to me. And that is a need which does not cease when it is met, and that in which the need finds fulfillment does not cease to be dear to me. That which pertains to me and to which I belong, is as reliable and constant for me as everything in my household. Socrates concludes that when someone loves another as a friend, his longing is directed to the other person in such a way that the former fulfills himself in his longing" (18–19). Gadamer's drawing attention to the element of hearing in belonging (*das Zugehoerige*) (19) is also suggestive in light of the title of Plutarch's essay.

On the role of the *oikos* as fundamental to Pindar's poetry, see Leslie Kurke, *The Traffic in Praise: Pindar and the Poetics of Social Economy* (Ithaca, 1991), esp. 15–61. Despite the title, Kurke does not treat *oikonomia* as a literary term.

34. For the pairing of *polutropos* and *poikilia* in the Scholia, see, e.g., Eustathius, *Commentarii ad Homeri Odysseam*, vol. 1 (Leipzig, 1825), 4; Heath, *Unity in Greek Poetics*, 109; and N. J. Richardson, "Homeric Professors in the Age of the Sophists," *Proceedings of the Cambridge Philological Society* 21 (1975): 65–81, esp. 79–80. For *atopos* as the opposite of *oikeion* in the scholia, see Dawson, *Allegorical Readers and Cultural Revision in Ancient Alexandria*, 65–71, and Heath, *Unity in Greek Poetics*, 102ff.; and in Plutarch, see, e.g., 18F, 27E, and 32F. On weaving and deception in the etymology of Penelope's name, see *A Commentary on Homer's Odyssey*, vol. 3, edited by Joseph Russo, Manuel Fernandez-Galiano, and Alfred Heubeck (Oxford, 1992), 80–81.

tales of others. But to be a cautious listener is not to be deprived altogether of listening. Considering and rejecting this more extreme precaution at the opening of his essay, Plutarch draws an explicit comparison between Homer's hero and the young reader: "Shall we then stop the ears of the young, as those of the Ithacans were stopped, with a hard and unyielding wax, and force them to put to sea in the Epicurean boat, and avoid poetry and steer their course clear of it; or rather shall we set them against some upright standard of reason and there bind them fast, guiding and guarding their judgment, that it may not be carried away from the course by pleasure towards that which will do them hurt?" [15D]. Unlike his crew, Odysseus experiences the pleasure of the Sirens' song, and he does so without the painful consequences, exactly the program Plutarch recommends for his youngster. For through the sweetness of poetry lies philosophy, and philosophy, as we have seen, is the goal. So Plutarch ends his essay hopeful of his students' progress.

Ending as he began, moreover, Plutarch articulates this intellectual journey from poetry to philosophy in Odyssean terms. In keeping with his arguments for the proper role of fiction in the curriculum, however, he replaces the dangerously seductive Sirens with the accommodating Phaeacians as the image of poetry:

> Wherefore, both because of these considerations and
> because of those already adduced, the young man has
> need of good pilotage (*agathēs kubernēseōs*) in the
> matter of reading, to the end that, forestalled with
> schooling (*propaideutheis*) rather than prejudice, in a
> spirit of friendship (*philos*) and goodwill (*eumenēs*)
> and familiarity (*oikeios*), he may be convoyed
> (*propempētai*) by poetry into the realm of philosophy.
> (37B)[35]

For Quintilian on Odysseus as *the* orator, see 12.10.64. For Odysseus as the image of the wise king in Philodemus, see Asmis, "Philodemus's Poetic Theory and *On the Good King According to Homer*," 39–45.

35. The Phaeacians represent—like fiction itself, a mixture of truth and falsity—a middle ground between the wholly fabulous creatures of books 1–8 and the wholly familiar Ithacans. On the nature of the Phaeacians, see Asmis, "Philodemus's Poetic Theory and *On the*

Like Odysseus on his journey home, the student also requires gentle convoy. Odysseus relies on the Phaeacians, legendary not only for their skillful piloting but also for their fictionality (see, e.g., *Odyssey* 8.555–66, 13.174). The young student, in turn, relies on fiction itself, whose soft, reflected light (*malakē augē*), in contrast to the direct rays of philosophy, echoes the softness (*malakia*) also traditionally attributed to these fictional seafarers and pointedly noticed by Plutarch (20A, cf. 27B; and see *Odyssey* 8.246–49).[36]

Thus gently conveyed by fiction, the young reader approaches the end of his educational journey, like Odysseus, in a relation of familiarity and belonging. No longer a stranger to philosophy, he is, like the wanderer returned, a *philos* among *philoi*. And like the individual in a proper relation to commonality or community, he is *oikeios,* a part of the whole: at home.

Reading poetry for Plutarch, then, is a complex process of accommodation, taking into account both ethical and formal considerations. As part of the complete curriculum, poetry serves only when properly accommodated to the curriculum as a whole, whose end and aim is philosophical understanding. Any passage or piece of poetry that fails to fit into this plan deserves exclusion not only from the whole text but ultimately from the whole educational program (cf. Quintilian 1.8.6). As a method of discourse, moreover, poetry accommodates human psychology, especially its attraction to variety and change as a source of pleasure. By approaching philosophy in this roundabout way, the student gradually becomes more comfortable and familiar with its truths.

Insofar as the poetry read belongs to an alien culture, like Homer's, the young student also depends on the strategies of accommodation institutionalized by the rhetorical and grammatical traditions for interpreting unfamiliar texts. As we have seen, two of these strategies, *decorum* and

---

Good King According to Homer," 35ff.; Charles Segal, "Bard and Audience in Homer," in *Homer's Ancient Readers,* edited by Lamberton and Keaney, 3–29; and *A Commentary on Homer's Odyssey,* vol. 1, edited by A. Heubeck, S. West, and J. B. Hainsworth (Oxford, 1988), 341–46.

On the movement of the argument toward a more positive view of poetry, see Schenkeveld, "The Structure of Plutarch's *De audiendis poetis,"* 62.

36. On the relation between *malakia* and such pastimes as story-telling, see *Nicomachean Ethics* 7.7.7–8.

oeconomia, render proper (*prepēs*) and fitting (*oikeia*) not only an alien truth but also an alien past. Plutarch's reader, then, faces the double odyssey of the philosopher and the grammarian: coming to feel at home in—that is, quite literally, accommodating—the bright light of philosophy, on one hand, and, on the other, the dim reflections of poetry's past.

CHAPTER THREE

Patristic Hermeneutics

From *scriptum* to *scriptura*

In the first book of the *Institutio Oratoria*, as we have seen in the previous chapter, Quintilian not only establishes the curriculum for grammatical training as a propaedeutic for rhetoric but institutionalizes, as a foundational part of this curriculum, literary interpretation or exegesis: what he calls *enarratio poetarum*. At the same time, Quintilian singles out as the two most important interpretive or exegetical strategies in this training *decorum* and *oeconomia* (1.8.17). Only fully characterized later in the *Institutio* as part of the rhetorician's art, these strategies, introduced at the outset, also figure prominently in the grammarian's art. Key principles of composition, in other words, they are also key principles of interpretation or reception. Indeed, as I suggested in chapter 2 and will develop here, these two principles, *decorum* and *oeconomia*, underlie the hermeneutical concept of contextualization, historical and textual, respectively.

As we have also seen, at least one influential grammarian and near contemporary of Quintilian conceptualizes reading the poets—*exēgēsis poiē tōn*—as a journey. Taking Odysseus's struggle to reach home as paradigmatic, Plutarch understands reading as a process of rendering the text familiar. Literary interpretation is in this radical sense a process of accommodation, of making oneself at home; and *decorum* and *oeconomia*, as rhetorical and grammatical instruments of accommodation, figure prominently in this process.

Both the instruments of accommodation themselves and the model of reading they affirm undergo renewal as part of the larger Christian appropriation of so-called classical culture. In this chapter I shall consider the hermeneutics of two especially influential advocates of appropriation,

Basil of Caesarea and Augustine of Hippo. Both men trained in the schools of grammar and rhetoric, and both worked as professional rhetoricians before becoming Fathers of the Church.[1] Their roughly contemporary adaptations of the principles of rhetorical and grammatical interpretation are epitomized in two especially influential tracts, Basil's *Address to Young Men on How to Use Greek Literature* and Augustine's *On Christine Doctrine*.

Together, these two works provide a telling glimpse of not only the diversity but also the underlying commonality of patristic hermeneutics in the early Eastern and Western Churches. Whereas Basil openly grounds his hermeneutics in a broadened concept of rhetorical *oikonomia*, Augustine, everywhere advocating *decorum*, builds his somewhat more indirectly on the strategies of rhetorical *interpretatio scripti*.

In the rhetorical and grammatical schools of the fourth century, *oikonomia* still reigns as a principle of composition and interpretation. On one hand, rhetoricians refer to it in praising the more artificial arrangement of material, Quintilian's *mos Homericus;* on the other, grammarians regularly apply it to moments in the narrative or dramatic action of a literary text that seem unfitting or inappropriate when read in isolation but entirely appropriate and artistic in the context of the work as a whole.[2]

1. See Robert A. Kaster, *Guardians of Language: The Grammarian and Society in Late Antiquity* (Berkeley, 1988), 72–74; Henri-Irénée Marrou, *A History of Education in Antiquity,* translated by George Lamb (New York, 1956), 314–29; Jaroslav Pelikan, *Christianity and Classical Culture: The Metamorphosis of Natural Theology in the Christian Encounter with Hellenism* (New Haven, 1993), 3–21; and Frances Young, "The Rhetorical Schools and Their Influence on Patristic Exegesis," *The Making of Orthodoxy: Essays in Honor of Henry Chadwick,* edited by Rowan Williams (Cambridge, 1989), 182–99.

2. See, e.g., Sulpitius Victor, *Institutiones Oratoriae,* ch. 14, in *Rhetores Latini Minores,* edited by C. Halm (Leipzig, 1863), 320. See also *Servii Grammatici in Vergilii carmina commentarii,* edited by G. Thilo and H. Hagen, 3 vols. (Leipzig, 1881), e.g., 5:45; 9:761, 9:593, 12:357, and *Aeli Donati Commentum Terenti,* edited by P. Wessner (Stuttgart, 1962), e.g., An. 459, En. 440, Ph. 534, 750.

For *oikonomia* as a strategy in biblical exegesis, including that of Philo and Irenaeus, see J. Reumann, "οἰκονομία as 'Ethical Accommodation' in the Fathers, and Its Pagan Backgrounds," *Studia Patristica* 3 (1961): 370–79, esp. 375: "In the second century A.D. *oikonomia* regularly denoted in these schools of rhetoric contemporary with Papias, Justin and Irenaeus an artificial order adopted for the sake of expediency to win a case." For Paul's influential use of this term, see esp. Eph. 3:2 and 3:9–10; J. Reumann, "OIKONOMIA-terms in Paul in Comparison with Lucan *Heilsgeschichte,*" *New Testament Studies* 13 (1966–67), 147–67, esp. 152–53; and Roos Meijering, *Literary and Rhetorical Theories in Greek Scholia* (Groningen, 1987), 171–200.

Both exegetical commentaries and rhetorical manuals, in other words, continue to acknowledge the economy of the most accomplished works of literature.

In this fourth-century setting, Basil, son of a rhetorician, turns from the grammatical and rhetorical schools, where he has been both a student (c. 351–55) and a teacher (355–56), to the Church, reckoning this concept of *oikonomia* among his traveling supplies, or *ephodia*, as he liked to call the pagan literary tradition in the possession of the Christian pilgrim (*Ad adolescentes* 10.3, 5).[3] Indeed, Basil is renowned for his application of this principle of *oikonomia*—not, however, to any literary text but rather to the theological controversies of his time.

One of the most pressing of these controversies concerns the divinity of the Holy Spirit. Gregory of Nazianzus, Basil's intimate friend, recounts an episode in this debate. On the occasion of a dinner party, Basil, being absent from the festivities, is in absentia criticized by one of the guests for having in a recent public sermon accommodated his personal view that the Holy Spirit is co-equal with the Father and the Son to the prevailing view of the Church for subordination. In his absent friend's defense, Gregory insists that Basil has wisely exercised *economy* in the interest of unity, whereas Basil's critic, characterized as an inflexible advocate of a minority view, would have Basil cling rigidly—or, as Gregory claims disapprovingly, with *akribeia*—to an unpopular opinion.[4]

3. On the details of Basil's career, see R. J. Deferrari, *The Letters*, 4 vols., Loeb Classical Library (London, 1934), 1:15–40, and Paul Jonathan Fedwick, "A Chronology of the Life and Works of Basil of Caesarea," in *Basil of Caesarea, Christian, Humanist, Ascetic: A Sixteen-Hundredth Anniversary Symposium*, vol. 1 (Toronto, 1981), 3–19. For text and translation of the *Ad adolescentes* I have used, with some modification, Deferrari, *The Letters*, 4:379–435.

4. See *Ep.* 58, PG 37, 113A–117B, and George L. Kustas, "Saint Basil and the Rhetorical Tradition," in *Basil of Caesarea*, edited by Fedwick, 1:221–79, esp. 223, 231–33. On the opposition of *oikonomia* to *akribeia* as analogous to that between rhetoric and philosophy, see ibid., 225–30. For the distinction between *oikonomia* and *theologia*, see Pelikan, *Christianity and Classical Culture*, 263–79. See also John H. Erickson, "*Oikonomia* in Byzantine Canon Law," *Law, Church, and Society: Essays in Honor of Stephan Kuttner*, edited by Kenneth Pennington and Robert Somerville (Philadelphia, 1977), 225–36; Ladislas Orsy, "In Search of the Meaning of *Oikonomia:* Report on a Convention," *Theological Studies* 43 (1982): 312–19, esp. 315; and André de Halleux, "'Oikonomia' in the First Canon of Saint Basil," *Patristic and Byzantine Review* 6 (1987): 53–64, esp. 56: "The essential meaning of the Orthodox definition of οἰκονομία may be found in the terms of this opposition to ἀκρίβεια." See, in addition, Jaroslav Pelikan, "The 'Spiritual Sense' of Scripture," in *Basil of Caesarea*, edited by Fedwick, 1:337–60.

In another of these controversies, Basil himself claims that some of his Asian predecessors had accepted controversial baptisms for reasons of economy. Without faulting their judgments, Basil nevertheless reaffirms in this circumstance the delicate balance between the priority of the whole and the integrity of the part:

> Accordingly I think that, since nothing has been clearly established regarding them, it is proper for us to reject their baptism, and if anyone has received it from them, to baptize him on his entering the Church. If, however, this shall prove to be injurious to the economy of the whole (*tēi katholou oikonomiai*), we must resort again to custom, and must follow those fathers who have economized on this matter concerning us (*tois oikonomēsasi ta kath' hēmas patrasin*). For I entertain some fear lest, while we desire to make the people cautious about baptizing, we may by the severity of our decision stand in the way of those who are being saved. But if they maintain our baptism, let this not disturb us. For we are not under obligation to return them the favor, but to observe the canons scrupulously (*akribeiai*). [*Ep.* 188, LCL, 3:18–19]

In this first canonical letter, Basil skillfully weighs the benefits of *oikonomia* against the demands of *akribeia*. Practically speaking, *oikonomia* entails making accommodations to the psychological needs of each individual believer in the service of a unified Christian community. Here as in Quintilian, it subordinates the means to a greater end, a part to the whole. *Akribeia*, by contrast, upholds strict adherence to some precise formulation or precedent, that is, not in adherence to the spirit but merely to the letter of the law.[5]

Although Basil invests this opposition between *oikonomia* and *akribeia*

---

5. See Orsy, "In Search of the Meaning of *Oikonomia*," 313: "The need for *oikonomia* arises when there is an apparent conflict between the claim of the law and the call of the Christian spirit." The opposition between law and spirit is taken up in more detail below.

with renewed power to advocate the most pressing concerns of his contemporaries, becoming, as he is still called, the Father of Economy,[6] both
the terms themselves and even their relation to one another are far from
innovative. As we have seen, they constitute the stock-in-trade of ancient
literary, legal, and, more generally, ethical analysis. At least as far back as
Aristotle, the rigidity, or *akribeia*, of the written law is opposed to the
accommodative function of equity.[7]

Designed to correct the injurious *akribeia* of legal statute by taking into
account the infinite variety of particular circumstance, equity, or *epieikeia*,
subordinates the words of the law to the legislator's intention, the act
committed to the agent's intention, and the part to the whole (see above,
12–16). The economical and equitable interpretation of texts and events
are alike, then, in resisting rigidity and partiality in favor of flexibility, generality, accommodation, and integrity or wholeness. The peculiar history
of the Church shares in preserving this early affiliation between these two
concepts in that *oikonomia*, an operative principle in the Eastern Church
since Basil's day, finds its long-standing counterpart in the Western Church
in the principle of *epieikeia*.[8]

6. See Halleux, "'Oikonomia' in the First Canon of Saint Basil," 53–64; K. Duchatelez,
"La notion d'économie et ses richesses théologiques," *Nouvelle revue théologique* 92 (1970):
267–92; and Constantine N. Tsirpanlis, "Doctrinal 'Oikonomia' and Sacramental
Koinonia in Greek Patristic Theology and Contemporary Orthodox Ecumenism," *Patristic and Byzantine Review* 6 (1987): 30–43, esp. 31–32: "Of course, Saint Basil the Great
was the *par excellence* "Father" of the "sacramental oikonomia" and had introduced the
expression οἰκονομίας ἕνεκα τῶν πολλῶν. He supported the recognition of the baptism of the Cathari accepted by some in Asia 'as a matter of accommodation with the
many' implying salvation of many souls. The first and second canonical letters of St. Basil
are the foundations of the Eastern Church *oikonomia*." See also R. A. Markus, "Trinitarian
Theology and the Economy," *Journal of Theological Studies*, n.s., 9 (1958): 89–102, and G. L.
Prestige, *God in Patristic Thought* (London, 1952), 57–67, 97–111.
7. For an early juxtaposition of *epieikōs* with *akribōs*, see Isocrates *Helen* 5; Kathy Eden,
Poetic and Legal Fiction in the Aristotelian Tradition (Princeton, 1986), 25–61; and Wesley
Trimpi, *Muses of One Mind: The Literary Analysis of Experience and Its Continuity* (Prince-
ton, 1983), 116–43, 235–40.
8. See John Reumann, "The 'Righteousness of God' and the 'Economy of God': Two
Great Doctrinal Themes Historically Compared," *A Festschrift for Archbishop Methodios of
Thyateira and Great Britain* (Thyateira, 1985), 615–37; Orsy, "In Search of the Meaning of
Oikonomia," esp. 316–17; and Erickson, "*Oikonomia* in Byzantine Canon Law," esp. 228,
where his characterization of *oikonomia* sounds very like Aristotle's of equity: "The sympa-
thy, philanthropy and condescension to be demonstrated by the steward of souls are not sim-

Basil's understanding of the role of *oikonomia* in theological matters corresponds to his application of this same concept to literary matters. Indeed, his *Address to Young Men Concerning How to Use Greek Literature,* the so-called *Ad adolescentes,* not only advocates an economical reception of the pagan literary tradition but offers a paradigm of this kind of reception in its reading of Plutarch's *De audiendis poetis.*[9] Whereas Plutarch, in ways outlined in the previous chapter, institutes poetry as a propaedeutic for philosophy because of its powers of accommodation, Basil encourages his young Christian wards, possibly his nephews, to read pagan literature, including poetry, history, and philosophy, as a propaedeutic for the study of Holy Scripture, and for a similar reason.[10] Like Plutarch's poetry, pagan

---

ply human affections but imitate Christ, and the resulting 'economy' is not capricious or arbitrary but rather based on an objective assessment of the plight of the sinner and how to remedy his situation. The steward of souls is obliged to consider whether the sin itself was committed knowingly or out of ignorance or stupidity, deliberately or out of fear and compulsion. He must take into account the total fabric of who and what the individual sinner is: his condition in life, his age, his marital status, etc. And even more than these "prelapsarian" factors, he must assess the sinner's zeal for amendment of life, the sincerity of his repentance, and above all, whether he has given up his sin."

9. And this despite N. G. Wilson, concerning Basil's sources: "This no doubt included Plutarch as well, with whom B. shares a liking for arguments based on analogy and similes. But although Plutarch has written essays on 'The education of children' and 'Reading the poets'. . . I have not found enough verbatim similarities to prove with the same degree of certainty that B. was borrowing directly from Plutarch. This, however, might be explained by supposing that B. had read one of his sources more recently than the other" (Wilson, ed., *St. Basil on the Value of Greek Literature* [London, 1975], 12).

In contrast, Deferrari, *The Letters,* 4:367, notes Basil's frequent reference to Plutarch. See also 374, where Deferrari cites the 1623 edition of Basil's essay in a volume with Plutarch's *De legendis poetis;* and see Ernesto Valgiglio, "Basilio Magno *Ad Adulescentes* e Plutarco *De audiendis poetis,*" *Rivista di studi classici* 23 (1975): 67–86, and Frances Young, "The Rhetorical Schools and Their Influence on Patristic Exegesis," 87–88.

10. See Ann Moffatt, "The Occasion of St. Basil's *Address to Young Men,*" *Antichton* 6 (1972): 83–86, which dates the work during the school year, 362/3, and Wilson, ed., *St. Basil on the Value of Greek Literature,* 7–16, who dates it to the middle or late seventies (9).

For the long-standing relation between economy and accommodation, see Kustas, "Saint Basil and the Rhetorical Tradition," 227–33. He begins: "At the core of οἰκονομία is the notion of accommodation to circumstance, whether in the daily management of an estate, as originally, or in church affairs, or in God's providential concern for his creatures as seen in the Incarnation" (227–28). See also J. Reumann, "οἰκονομία as 'Ethical Accommodation' in the Fathers, and Its Pagan Backgrounds," 370–79; Duchatelez, "La notion d'économie et ses richesses théologiques," 267–92; and Erickson, "*Oikonomia* in Byzantine Canon Law," esp. 230–32.

literature, according to Basil, better accommodates the particular psychological needs of the young student:

> Yet so long as, by reason of your age, it is impossible
> for you to understand the depth of the meaning (*tēs
> dianoias*) of [Holy Scriptures], in the meantime, by
> means of other [writings] which are not entirely dif-
> ferent, we give, as it were in shadows and reflections,
> a preliminary training (*progymnazometha*) to the eye
> of the soul. . . . So we also . . . must associate with
> poets and writers of prose and orators and with all
> men from whom there is any prospect of benefit with
> reference to the care of our soul. . . . so we also in the
> same manner must first . . . be instructed by these out-
> side means, and then shall understand the sacred and
> mystical teachings; and like those who have become
> accustomed to seeing the reflection of the sun in
> water, so we shall then direct our eyes to the light
> itself. [2.6–8]

Recasting the preparatory exercises to accommodate Christian ends, Basil also reworks the metaphor of reflected, in contrast to direct, light that illuminates the progress (cf. 9.6).[11]

Furthermore, Basil argues in favor of making young Christians familiar with Greek *paideia* on the grounds of what he calls *oikeiotēs*, another word deriving ultimately from *oikos* but more immediately related to *oikeion*, that term so fundamental to Plutarch's pedagogical program, and for Basil inextricably linked to *oikonomia*.[12] Conveniently translated as

11. On *progymnazometha* as a technical term for preliminary training, see Wilson, ed., *St. Basil on the Value of Greek Literature*, 43, and George A. Kennedy, *Greek Rhetoric under Christian Emperors* (Princeton, 1983), 54–73; and for the image of reflected light, see Wilson, ed., *St. Basil on the Value of Greek Literature*, 44, and above, 34–35. For Basil's platonism, see John M. Rist, "Basil's 'Neoplatonism': Its Background and Nature," *Basil of Caesarea*, edited by Fedwick, 1:137–220. See also Kaster, *Guardians of Language*, 77–78.

12. See Kustas, "Saint Basil and the Rhetorical Tradition," esp. 253: "τὸ οἰκεῖον has roots deep in Greek culture. It marks a sense of belonging taken at its ideal and could be applied across a broad range of experience. Language in order to be effective requires the "right" style and the right choice of words; refinement and taste as cultural values depend on

"familiarity," the condition of being from the same *oikos*, *oikeiotēs* figures prominently in the three principal parts of Basil's argument. In each of these parts, as we shall see, he moreover colors his argument for familiarity with striking allusions to the *Odyssey*, most memorably the Sirens and the Phaeacians. Like Plutarch, in other words, Basil imagines the interpreter's labors in terms of Odysseus's struggle to reach home.

---

a sense of fitness; and, in general, it could point the way for overcoming alienation and resolving conflict. For some Neoplatonists οἰκειότης becomes almost an obsession: it helped describe for them the transcendent unity after which they sought. Among Christians it is much in evidence in Origen. Finding equations is after all allegory's stock in trade. Furthermore, under its aegis individual and society can effectively interact, as in a monastic community, and in the clash between Christianity and classical culture it could signal the way to cooperation. Indeed, the *Ad adolescentes* is inspired by this very standard, the selection of what is suitable in the old for the purpose of forming the new Christian learning. In sum, οἰκειότης served as a kind of ethical touchstone, as a guide to action. For Basil in particular οἰκονομία is the right application and realization of τὸ οἰκεῖον."

On the close association of *to oikeion* and *to prepon* in Basil, see Kustas, "Saint Basil and the Rhetorical Tradition," 252–54, esp. 254: "It would not be much of an exaggeration to claim that οἰκεῖον/πρέπον or synonymous terminology appears on practically every page of Basil's writings. The emphasis is testimony to how deeply ingrained in him is the social instinct, the thirst for context, on which the conception is essentially based."

In "Christianity and Hellenism in Basil the Great's Address *Ad Adulescentes*," *Neoplatonism and Early Christian Thought: Essays in Honor of A. H. Armstrong* (London, 1981), 189–203, Ernest L. Fortin mentions *oikonomia*, which he identifies with lying, in the last two sentences, concluding: "Whether or not the strategy of spiritual warfare that they invented for this purpose entangled them in a web of complicated lies is a question which they themselves were understandably loath to raise and which they managed to circumvent by giving to the old art of lying a new and more felicitous label. They called it the 'economy of truth'. The expression dates from that period, but the unimpeachable Christian pedigree of the word *oikonomia* was enough to remove from it any taint of opprobrium and guarantee its success for a long time to come" (200).

This period of the flowering of Christian *oikonomia* is not accidentally also the period of the ecumenical councils; and it is worth remembering not only the origins of the concept *oikoumenē*, like *oikonomia*, in the *oikos* but also its traditional location in Homer's *Odyssey*. See on this matter Eric Voegelin, *Order and History*, vol. 4: *The Ecumenic Age* (Baton Rouge, 1974), 203: "In the Ecumenic Age, the older symbolism that had to yield to expanding knowledge was the *okeanos* as the boundary of the *oikoumenē*. In the time of the epics, the *okeanos* marks the horizon where Odysseus finds the Cimmerians and the entrance to the underworld of the dead (*Odyssey*, XI): it is the border of the *oikoumenē* beyond which lies the Islands of the Blessed (IV, 56 ff.). In the epics, this, the *oikoumenē* is not yet a territory to be conquered together with its population. The experience of the 'horizon' as the boundary between the visible expanse of the *oikoumenē* and the divine mystery of its being is still fully alive; and the integral symbolism of the *oikoumenē-okeanos* still expresses the In-between reality of the cosmos as a whole."

At once establishing his *ēthos* and capturing the goodwill of his audience, Basil opens his essay by asserting the familiarity between himself and his listeners or readers. On one hand, as he claims, he stands to them in a relation of *oikeiotēs* exceeded only by their natural fathers (1.2); and on the other, his advice derives from his vast experience of the world, a worldliness traditionally located in the figure of Odysseus.[13] After effecting this *captatio benevolentiae*, Basil concludes his introduction (1.5) with a direct quotation from book 8 of the *Odyssey* (l. 500), where the Phaeacian singer Demodokos begins his interpretation of the received material of the Trojan War with the words *enthen helōn*.[14] Invoking the singer of the Iliadic tradition, Basil uses these same words—*enthen helōn*—as he, too, undertakes to make an old tradition familiar to a new audience.

In the next section Basil moves from the *oikeiotēs* between himself and his audience to that between the tradition of holy writing and the pagan literary tradition, offering as an appropiate and familiar illustration—what he calls a *paradeigma oikeioteron*—the relation between soul and body (2.5).[15] For "if there is some affinity (*oikeiotēs*) between the two bodies of

---

13. *Odyssey* 1.3. In *Ep.* 74, Basil quotes this very line not only in praise of the addressee, Martinianus, but also in defense of education: "For if it is important as a proof of education 'to have seen the cities of many men and to have learned their minds,' this boon is, I think, conferred in a short time by converse with you. For what superiority is there in seeing many men one by one over seeing one single person who has taken to himself the experience of all mankind?" (2:69). He then complicates the reference, featuring himself as Alcinous, content to listen to Odysseus's (i.e., Martinianus's) tale not only for a year but for the rest of his life. See also *Ep.* 186 (3:3–4) and *Ep.* 14, where his retreat on the Pontus is compared to Calypso's island (1:107–9). See also Kustas, "Saint Basil and the Rhetorical Tradition," 277, who describes Odysseus as "the epitome in the classical tradition of socially responsive, prudent, intellectual, ethical and rhetorical man."

For Melanchthon on the role of Odysseus as the man of experience in a encomiastic declamation about Basil, see *De Basilio Episcopo* (1545), in *Corpus Reformatorum* (hereafter *CR*), edited by C. G. Bretschneider, 28 vols. (Halle, 1843), 11:677.

14. See Wilson, ed., *St. Basil on the Value of Greek Literature*, 40. It is also possible that his reference at 1.5 to "the rudders of your mind, as if of a ship" echoes the Phaeacian ships at *Odyssey* 8.555–63. For other references in this essay to the *Odyssey*, the single most cited text, see 4.4, 4.10, 6.1, and 9.26. On the role of Homer more generally in the traditions of late antiquity, see Robert Lamberton, *Homer the Theologian: Neoplatonist Allegorical Reading and the Growth of the Epic Tradition* (Berkeley, 1986).

15. See 9.12–18, where Basil further develops the relation of body to soul, and *De doctrina* 1.23.22–1.26.27, where Augustine uses this relation to illuminate that between the literal and spiritual interpretation of Scripture. See below, 56–62.

teachings," he claims, "knowledge of them should be useful to us" (3.1). Here he advances the propaedeutic value of pagan literature, citing as examples Moses, who progressed from the learning of the Egyptians to "contemplation of Him who is," and Daniel, who began, no less usefully, with the wisdom of the Chaldeans. But even granting this propaedeutic value in principle, the Christian interpreter still needs an interpretive *praxis*.

To formulate this *praxis*, Basil once again forges his position out of Plutarchan material, not only borrowing the traditional figure of the bee from the *De audiendis* and elsewhere (32 EF; cf. *Moralia* 79 CD) but, more important for our purposes, also adapting the episode of the Sirens (4.2–3); only in the Basilian appropriation, the reader imitates an Odysseus who, rather like his crew in the Homeric original and the Plutarchan adaptation, avoids altogether the temptation of seductive song: "[B]ut when they treat of wicked men, you ought to avoid such imitation, stopping your ears no less than Odysseus did, according to what those same poets say, when he avoided the songs of the Sirens. For familiarity (*sunētheia*) with evil words is, as it were, a road leading to evil deeds" (4.2–3).[16] Even while appropriating from the literature what is, in Basil's words, *oikeion hēmin* (4.8)— suitable or appropriate to us—we are advised to pass over the rest. And what is appropriate to us is virtue, or *aretē*. "For it is no small advantage," Basil claims, "that a certain intimacy (*oikeiotēta*) and familiarity (*sunētheian*) with virtue should be engendered in the souls of the young, seeing that the lessons leavened by such are likely, in the nature of the case, to be indelible, having been deeply impressed in them by reason of the tenderness of their souls" (5.1–2).

In the remainder of the essay, then, Basil both amplifies this third relation of *oikeiotēs*, that between the soul and virtue, and demonstrates for the young reader how the best of pagan literature, when properly interpreted, enforces this relation. Not surprisingly, for illustration Basil turns to the *Odyssey*, in particular to the episode of Odysseus among the Phaeacians:

---

16. See Wilson, ed., *St. Basil on the Value of Greek Literature*, 47, who, citing the Plutarchan adaptation, notes no difference between it and Basil's. In contrast, see Fortin, "Christianity and Hellenism in Basil the Great's Address *Ad Adulescentes*," 190, and Valgiglio, "Basilio Magno *Ad Adulescentes* e Plutarco *De audiendis poetis*," 68.

Moreover, as I myself have heard a man say who is clever (*deinou*) at understanding a poet's mind (*poiētou dianoian*), all Homer's poetry is an encomium of virtue, and all he wrote, save what is accessory, bears to this end, and not least in those verses in which he has portrayed the leader of the Cephallenians, after being saved from shipwreck, as naked, and the princess as having first shown him reverence, at the mere sight of him (so far was he from incurring shame through merely being seen naked, since the poet has portrayed him as clothed with virtue in place of garments), and then, furthermore, Odysseus as having been considered worthy of such high honor by the rest of the Phaeacians likewise that, disregarding the luxury in which they lived, they one and all admired and envied the hero, and none of the Phaeacians at the moment would have desired anything else more than to become Odysseus, and that too just saved from a shipwreck. For in these passages, the interpreter of the poet's mind (*ho tou poiētou tēs dianoias exēgētēs*) was wont to declare that Homer says in a voice that all but shouts: "You must give heed unto virtue, O men, which swims forth even with a man who has suffered shipwreck, and, on his coming naked to land, will render him more honoured than the happy Phaeacians." And truly this is so. [5.6–9; cf. 5.12, 6.1]

Faced with the arguably unseemly events at Phaeacia, from the encounter between the naked Odysseus and Nausicaa to the depiction of Phaeacian pastimes, Basil's anonymous exegete, unidentifiable as either pagan or Christian, interprets this Homeric episode economically, in the manner of Quintilian's *grammaticus*.[17] He reads it, like Socrates reading Simonides in

17. See Wilson, ed., *St. Basil on the Value of Greek Literature*, 52. For the aim of literary interpretation and its relation to scriptural interpretation, including the role of charity (*agapē*), see *Ep.* 104 (3:155–75), esp. 165–69.

the *Protagoras*, for the poet's *dianoia*, or intention, where intentionality implies some general aim or overall purpose (cf. 5.12). Whereas Simonides' intention was refutation, however, Homer's is teaching virtue. And Homer, the most excellent of poets and father of the *mos Homericus*, has so arranged his poem that all the parts accommodate this intention, challenging the interpreter to uncover and appreciate its economy.

Like his anonymous exegete, Basil, too, reads the works of the past economically. And this includes, as we have seen, Plutarch as well as Homer. Both of these pagan authors, in Basil's view, not only familiarize the young reader with the aim of all learning—virtue, or *aretē*—but they also address the all-important process of accommodation involved in making something one's own.[18] Homer's hero reaches home after long journeying only by accommodating each new circumstance; Plutarch's exegete approaches philosophical understanding as the end of all his or her reading not only by first experiencing the accommodative powers of fiction but by skillfully interpreting these fictions with the help of such strategies of accommodation as *decorum* and *oikonomia*. Accommodating both Homer and Plutarch to his own Christian aims, Basil counsels his young readers (or listeners) to familiarize themselves not only with these authors but with

---

For the image of the *oikonomos* as *kubernētēs*, and accommodation as a kind of pilotage in ways reminiscent of the role of the Phaeacians both in Homer and in Plutarch, see Erickson, "*Oikonomia* in Byzantine Canon Law," 230: "We now see the *oikonomos* as *kubernētēs*, as the pilot of a ship at sea, relaxing the tiller to avoid capsize, jetisoning what is less important to save the cargo, or steering between the scylla and charybdis of the day. *Oikonomia* in this sense of accommodation frequently occurs not only in secular but also in patristic literature, particularly in biblical exegesis, where the word is used to describe otherwise embarrassing incidents, like Paul's circumcision of Timothy. In addition, appeals to this *oikonomia*/accommodation were not absent from the world of ecclesiastical affairs, at least from the mid-fourth century on: in a church racked by theological controversies, some accommodation in dealing with the multitudes in some way tainted by schism or heresy increasingly became a matter of necessity."

18. For medieval views of reading, more generally, as a process of *familiariʒation* or *domestication*, see Mary J. Carruthers, *The Book of Memory: A Study of Memory in Medieval Culture* (Cambridge, 1990), esp. 164: "Perhaps no advice is as common in medieval writing on the subject, and yet so foreign, when one thinks about it, to the habits of modern scholarship as this notion of 'making one's own' what one reads in someone else's work. 'Efficere tibi illas familiares,' Augustine's admonition to 'Francesco,' does not mean 'familiar' in quite the modern sense. *Familiar* is rather a synonym of *domesticare*, that is, to make something familiar by making it a part of your own experience." Of course, *domus* is the Latin equivalent of the Greek *oikos*.

the whole literary tradition from which they come. Having made this tradition their own, he contends, these Christian youths will be well launched on their own spiritual journeys home.

Like Basil, Augustine figures reading as a journey and reading well as the journey home. Indeed, the *De doctrina christiana,* Augustine's instructions to the Christian on what and how to read, imagines the activity as an odyssey, one, like Plutarch's image of reading, potentially full of danger: "Suppose we were wanderers (*peregrini*) who could not live in blessedness except at home (*patria*), miserable in our wandering (*peregrinatione*) and desiring to end it and to return to our native country. We would need vehicles (*vehiculis*) for land and sea which could be used to help us reach our homeland, which is to be enjoyed. But if the amenities (*amoenitates*) of the journey and the motion (*gestatio*) of the vehicles itself delighted us, and we were led (*conversi*) to enjoy those things which we should use, we should not wish to end our journey (*viam*) quickly, and entangled in a perverse sweetness (*perversa suavitate*), we should be alienated from our country (*alienaremur a patria*), whose sweetness would make us blessed" (1.4.4).[19]

Worrying, in contrast to Plutarch, more about the subtle lure of Phaeacian hospitality than the open seduction of the Sirens' song, Augustine cautions against taking the way home for home itself—*via* for *patria*. And whereas the Plutarchan essay figures the accommodative power of fiction, as a propaedeutic for philosophy, in the fictional and fiction-loving Phaea-

19. On the role of grammatical training, the propaedeutic for rhetorical training, in Augustine's hermeneutics, see Henri-Irénée Marrou, *Saint Augustin et la fin de la culture antique* (Paris, 1938); Kaster, *Guardians of Language,* 84–88; Peter Brown, *Augustine of Hippo* (Berkeley, 1967), 35–40, 259–69; and Irvine, *The Making of Textual Culture,* 169–89.

For the role of rhetorical training, see Charles Sears Baldwin, *Medieval Rhetoric and Poetic* (New York, 1928), 51–73; Kathy Eden, "The Rhetorical Tradition and Augustinian Hermeneutics in *De doctrina christiana,*" *Rhetorica* 8 (1990): 45–63; George A. Kennedy, *Classical Rhetoric and Its Christian and Secular Tradition* (Chapel Hill, 1950), 153–57; James J. Murphy, "Saint Augustine and the Debate about a Christian Rhetoric," *Quarterly Journal of Speech* 46 (1960): 400–410, and *Rhetoric in the Middle Ages* (Berkeley, 1974), 43–88; and Gerald A. Press, "The Subject and Structure of Augustine's *De doctrina christiana,*" *Augustiniana* 31 (1981): 165–82, and "*Doctrina* in Augustine's *De doctrina christiana,*" *Philosophy and Rhetoric* 17 (1984): 98–115.

For quotations of the text of the *De doctrina christiana* in Latin I have used *Oeuvres de Saint Augustin,* vol. 11, edited by G. Combès and Farges (Paris, 1949); for those in English, *On Christian Doctrine,* translated by D. W. Robertson (Indianapolis, 1958).

cian seafarers, Augustine transfers this power of accommodation to the figure of Christ. For having accommodated himself to our humanity (1.14.13, cf. 1.12.12), he is at once the vehicle of the journey and its destination. "Although he is our native country (*patria*)," Augustine explains early in book 1, "He made himself also the Way (*viam*) to that country" (1.11.11). Combining, as it were, the Plutarchan roles of poetry and philosophy, Christ is at once "the way" and "the truth" (1.34.38). He provides not only for those arriving at their estate but also, as the propaedeutic, for those just preparing to set out on the journey (1.34.38).

Thus cautioned about the dangers of failing to distinguish between the way home and home itself, the exegete must also beware the habit of taking alternate routes—*transversa* and *perversa* (1.36.41). Even though such deviating ultimately leads to the same destination, defined exegetically as the overall intention of Scripture, it nevertheless misinterprets the author's meaning in the particular passage under consideration. And these local misreadings, Augustine warns, also pose a serious threat: "In asserting rashly that which the author before him did not intend (*non sensit*), he may find many other passages which he cannot reconcile (*contexere*) with his interpretation. If he acknowledges these to be true and certain, his first interpretation cannot be true, and under these conditions it happens, I know not why, that, loving his own interpretation, he begins to become angrier with the Scriptures than he is with himself " (1.37.41). In describing here the errant interpreter's frustration, Augustine takes for granted not only the standard of authorial intention but the hermeneutical expectation of the integrity or wholeness of Scripture based on that intention—its *oeconomia*, in the terminology of ancient rhetoric and grammar. He takes for granted, in other words, the subordination of the parts to the whole; and he describes in turn the interpreter's gradual reception of these individual passages as parts of a larger whole with the verb *contexere:* to weave together. Like *oeconomia* and *decorum*, as we saw in chapter 2, the analogy between weaving and discourse serves literary reception as well as literary composition. To interpret Scripture, for Augustine, is in effect to weave its meaning.

Augustine, then, inherits not only the traditional analogy between reading and the journey home but also that between the literary work read and a carefully woven tapestry (see above, 35–37). Indeed, throughout the *De doctrina,* Augustine prescribes the concept of *context*—not only textual but also historical—as a remedy against scriptural obscurity, relying for his prescriptions on a specialized terminology, including *textus, contextus, contextio,* and *circumstantia.*

So in cases of obscurity caused by ambiguity, either in the original language or in some translation, Augustine advises the practicing exegete to apply the same strategy that Cicero recommends to the rhetorician in training: "But if both meanings, or all of them, in the event that there are several, remain ambiguous after the faith has been consulted, then it is necessary to examine the context (*textus ipse*) of the preceding and following parts (*a praecedentibus et consequentibus partibus*) surrounding the ambiguous place, so that we may determine which of the meanings among those which suggest themselves it would allow to be consistent (*contexi*)" (3.2.2).[20] Some readings, in other words, are more neatly and easily interwoven than others with the existing fabric of meaning.

Like Cicero in the *De inventione,* however, Augustine considers not only the immediate textual context—the *partes praecedentes et consequentes* —but also the work as a whole, what Cicero had called *omnis scriptura* (*De inventione* 2.40.117) and what Augustine, as we shall see, understands as the *summa* of Scripture, or *caritas.* And like Cicero, Augustine also recommends considering the whole set of circumstances that inform the composition—times, places, persons, and so on (3.12.19, 3.20.29).

The rhetorical and grammatical traditions, as we have seen in previous chapters, call this principle *decorum* as it applies to composition. As a principle of interpretation, it constitutes the historical context; and Augustine refers to it in one place simply as *historia* (2.28.42) and in another as *circumstantia.*[21] Alongside textual context, and in league with *collatio locorum* and a knowledge of the text in its original language, historical context works to resolve ambiguity: "Only rarely and with difficulty may we find

---

20. Cf. *De doctrina* 2.12.18, 2.14.21, 3.2.5, 3.3.6, 3.28.39, 3.37.55; and see above, 17–18.

21. Under *historia* Augustine includes natural history and human history. See 2.28.44–46. For the place of history in the grammatical tradition, see above, 26–27. At *De musica* 2.1.1, Augustine calls grammar the *custodia historiae.* For the place of history in the rhetorical tradition, see, e.g., *De oratore* 1.5.18, 1.34.158, 2.9.36, 2.12.53.

On the *circumstantiae,* see Augustine's *De rhetorica* ch. 7, and Isidore's *De rhetorica* ch. 21, both in *Rhetores Latini Minores,* edited by Halm, 141, 517; and see above, 17–18.

ambiguities in the literal meanings (*ambiguitas in propriis verbis*) of scriptural vocabulary which may not be solved either by examining the [historical] context (*circumstantia*) which reveals the author's intention (*scriptorum intentio*), or by comparing translations (*interpretum collatio*), or by consulting a text in an earlier language" (3.4.8). While recalling the Ciceronian strategies of contextualization, Augustine's instructions on how to resolve ambiguity and establish authorial intention also recall the original context of Cicero's treatment of these strategies—namely, the topic of *interpretatio scripti*. Indeed, Augustinian hermeneutics, as expounded in the *De doctrina*, stands as a profound reading and reworking of the rhetorical tradition of interpretation straightforwardly preserved in Augustine's early rhetoric and outlined in chapter 1.[22]

Within this tradition, as we have seen, disputes arising over controversial texts rest most often on one of two grounds: the discrepancy between the writer's words and intention—so-called *scriptum* versus *voluntas*—and ambiguity. Whereas ambiguity is a feature of language, and more precisely its potential for multiple signification, intentionality is an ethical and legal concept. Treated under *elocutio*, or style, ambiguity looks to what words mean, while intention, treated under the proofs of invention, looks to what ethical and legal agents mean. Well aware of the practical overlapping of these grounds, rhetoricians, such as Cicero and Quintilian, insisted on keeping them separate, at least in theory.

Building on this tradition, which includes Augustine's own *De rhetorica*, the hermeneutics of the *De doctrina* is founded not only on these two grounds of controversy but also on their theoretical separateness. Although *scriptum* is narrowed to the more specialized *scriptura* and *voluntas* is expanded to include the will of the interpreter and even the *signa* he interprets, the opposition in its legal formulation underlies the opposition between spiritual and carnal or corporeal reading introduced in the first book and developed throughout.[23] This Christianization of rhetorical interpretation-theory, however, is Paul's doing, not Augustine's.

22. In his early *De rhetorica* ch. 11, Augustine refers specifically to the four types of controversy or *quaestiones legales* of the rhetorical manuals: *scriptum et voluntas, contentio legum contrarium, ambiguitas,* and *conlectio* (ibid., 143). Cf. Cassiodorus *Institutiones* 2.2.4–6, in ibid., 496–97, and *An Introduction to Divine and Human Readings,* translated by Leslie Webber Jones (New York, 1969), 150–52.

23. On the central role of will, or *voluntas,* in Augustinian ethics, psychology, and

A Hellenized Jew with a good rhetorical education, Paul appropriates the opposition between *scriptum* and *voluntas*—in his Greek, *rhēton* and *dianoia*—but changes the terms to accommodate his Jewish constituency. A skilled rhetorician, Paul chooses terms familiar to Jewish law, reformulating the opposition from *scriptum* versus *voluntas* to *gramma* versus *pneuma*.[24] Augustine's Latin renders the Greek *gramma* versus *pneuma* as *littera* versus *spiritus*: letter versus spirit. The opposition between literal and spiritual reading, in other words, transforms the first ground of controversy from the rhetorical tradition of interpretation. Like *voluntas*, its older, rhetorical counterpart, spiritual interpretation looks beyond the letter or words themselves to the intention and beyond the part to the whole, even preserving, as we shall see, its long-standing alliance with equity.

For the exegete who reads Scripture spiritually—that is, for the *voluntas*, or intention—discovers that, with the same economy characteristic of the best pagan literature, all its parts accommodate the whole; and the whole or general intention of the divine *scriptor* is the promotion of *caritas* and the eradication of *cupiditas* (3.10.15). *Caritas*, in other words, is the *summa* of all scriptural teaching (cf. 1.35.39);[25] and as both the *voluntas* of

hermeneutics, see Albrecht Dihle, *The Theory of Will in Classical Antiquity* (Berkeley, 1982), 123–44; Eden, *Poetic and Legal Fiction in the Aristotelian Tradition*, 120–40, and "The Rhetorical Tradition and Augustinian Hermeneutics in *De doctrina christiana*," 47–55; and Neal. W. Gilbert, "The Concept of Will in Early Latin Philosophy," *Journal of the History of Philosophy* 1 (1963): 32–33.

24. On this matter, see Boaz Cohen, *Jewish and Roman Law* (New York, 1966), 37–38, "Letter and Spirit in Jewish and Roman Law," *Mordecai M. Kaplan Jubilee Volume*, edited by Moshe Davis (New York, 1953), 109–35, and "Note on Letter and Spirit in the New Testament," *Harvard Theological Review* 47 (1954): 197–203. See also Alan F. Segal, *Paul the Convert* (New Haven, 1990), esp. 122–23. On the influence of classical rhetoric on Rabbinic methods of interpretation, see David Daube, "Rabbinic Methods of Interpretation and Hellenistic Rhetoric," *Hebrew Union College Annual* 22 (1949): 239–64, "Alexandrian Methods of Interpretation and the Rabbis," in *Essays in Greco-Roman and Related Talmudic Literature*, edited by Henry A. Fischel (New York, 1977), 165–82, and "Texts and Interpretation in Roman and Jewish Law," *Essays in Greco-Roman and Related Talmudic Literature*, 240–65; and Solomon Zeitlin, "Hillel and the Hermeneutic Rules," in *Studies in the Early History of Judaism*, vol. 1 (New York, 1973), 339–51.

25. In a hermeneutical context, *summa* is a technical term nearly synonymous with *voluntas* and *sententia;* and the traditional opposition between *verbatim* and *summatim*, whose alternative is *verbatim/sententialiter*, corresponds to the opposition between *scriptum* and *voluntas*. See, e.g., *Phaedrus* 288D, Seneca *Ep.* 100.12, and Carruthers, *Book of Memory*, 89–90. For the use of this term in humanist hermeneutics, see below, 84–85, 98.

Scripture, in contrast to its *scriptum* or *verba*, and the whole, in contrast to the part, *caritas* represents the Christianization of *aequitas*, or equity. Like equity, charity corrects the rigidity of the law—here Jewish law—by judging the agent's intentions rather than his or her actions. Like equity, charity accommodates human weakness, not only measuring any single event against the quality of our lives as a whole but also pitying and pardoning our errors.[26]

Augustine, then, outspokenly advocates a hermeneutics in which the meaning of the whole simultaneously depends on and informs the meaning of the parts. Though troubling to some students of the *De doctrina*, this circularity looks not only back to the rhetorical arguments and counterarguments for *scriptum* versus *voluntas* but ahead to the circle of understanding at the center of modern hermeneutics. Indeed, a hermeneutics of charity defines a disposition toward the text rather than any doctrine, in that the discovery of *caritas* within the text not only finds support elsewhere—indeed, everywhere else—in the text but also qualifies the *voluntas* of the reader by qualifying his or her way of reading as equitable or, in Augustine's terms, spiritual in that it searches out the *voluntas* of the writer.[27]

In keeping with his warnings against other interpretive errors, moreover, Augustine also cautions against the reading that fails to search out the *voluntas*, or intention, of the *scriptor*, stopping short at his *scriptum* or *verba;* and he associates this error with the hermeneutical practice of the Jews. For clinging to the letter of the text, and thus to the signs themselves instead of what they signify, the Judaizing interpretation is literal in the sense of carnal or corporeal (see 3.6.10, 3.7.11). "Nor is there anything more appropriately called the death of the soul," Augustine warns, "than that condition in which the thing which distinguishes us from beasts, which

---

26. Cf. Aristotle *Rhetoric* 1.13.15–19, and see Eden, *Poetic and Legal Fiction in the Aristotelian Tradition*, 136–39.

27. See *De trinitate* 15.20.38: *Nam quid est aliud caritas, quam voluntas.* For the circle of understanding in modern hermeneutics, see Hans-Georg Gadamer, *Truth and Method*, translated by Joel Weinsheimer and Donald G. Marshall (New York, 1989), 175–77, esp. 291–300, and David Couzens Hoy, *The Critical Circle: Literature, History and Philosophical Hermeneutics* (Berkeley, 1978). See also Gerald L. Bruns, "The Problem of Figuration in Antiquity," in *Hermeneutics: Questions and Prospects*, edited by Gary Shapiro and Alan Sica (Amherst, 1984), 147–64, esp. 157–64.

is the understanding, is subjected to the flesh in the pursuit of the letter (*sequendo litteram*)" (3.5.9).

Based, as we have seen, on the fundamentally legal formula *scriptum* versus *voluntas*, the opposition between literal and spiritual reading in the *De doctrina* is complicated—and recently even confused—by the overlapping of another opposition, literal (*propria*) versus figurative (*translata, figurata*), whose basis is not legal but stylistic. Whereas some scriptural passages signify literally, others also signify figuratively. In keeping with his rhetorical and grammatical training, however, Augustine fully appreciates not only the inherent capacity of language to signify in more than one way but also the ambiguities that arise from this multiple signification.[28]

For this reason, ambiguity, the second ground of controversy in *interpretatio scripti*, also constitutes a principal difficulty for the exegete of *scriptura*. Like the young student of *enarratio poetarum* and the interpreter of controversial legal *scripta*, the scriptural interpreter must learn to distinguish between literal and figurative or metaphorical expression; more precisely, Augustine insists, he must also learn to avoid not only taking figurative expressions as literal but, even more notably, taking literal expressions as figurative: "To this warning that we must beware not to take figurative (*figuratam*) or transferred (*translatam*) expressions as though they were literal (*propriam*), a further warning must be added lest we wish to take literal (*propriam*) expressions as though they were figurative (*figuratam*). Therefore a method of determining whether a locution is literal or figurative must be established" (3.10.14; cf. 3.5.9). And that method is the rule of charity. For, Augustine continues, if the interpreter discovers literally (*proprie*) in the text a meaning that accommodates the unified intention or *summa* of the *scriptor*, then the passage under consideration is not figurative (3.15.23).

Augustine, in other words, upholds the literal over the figurative reading whenever the former produces a spiritual interpretation, defined as an interpretation in keeping with charity as the intention, or *summa*, of the sacred text. Such a reading will necessarily be consistent with the textual context. In many cases, then, the spiritual (*spiritualis*) and the literal (*pro-*

---

28. For Augustine's earlier views on the relation between *obscuritas* and *ambiguitas*, see *De dialectica* 8.14–9.16.

pria) reading coincide. Whereas Augustine never advises the interpreter to read carnally (*carnaliter, corporaliter*), attending only to the words and not to the intention behind them, he finds ample occasion for reading literally (*proprie*). Accommodating rhetorical interpretation-theory to Christian ends, Augustinian hermeneutics in the *De doctrina* on one hand incorporates both legal and stylistic strategies for explicating controversial texts and on the other safeguards the distinction between them.[29]

That Augustine intends to distinguish the spiritual/corporeal–literal opposition from the figurative/literal opposition is confirmed by his extended treatment of Tyconius's *Liber Regularum* (3.30.42–3.37.56), which, according to Augustine, makes the same separation even though it advances a somewhat different terminology.[30] The opposition between spirit and letter, so crucial to his own hermeneutics, Augustine explains, corresponds in Tyconius to "Of Promises and the Law" (3.33.46); and this opposition, formulated as a rule, stands apart from all the other rules, which, according to Augustine, treat figurative (*tropica*) expression:

> All of these rules except one, which is called "Of
> Promises and the Law," cause one thing to be under-
> stood from another, a situation proper to figurative
> locutions (*tropicae locutionis*). The scope of such
> expressions, it seems to me, is too broad for any one
> man to comprehend entirely. For wherever one
> wishes to say one thing so that another is understood,

29. Cf. *De catechizandis rudibus* 26.50, and see James Samuel Preus, *From Shadow to Promise: Old Testament Interpretation from Augustine to the Young Luther* (Cambridge, Mass., 1969), 9–23, esp. 14: "There is much potential for confusion in this. 'Literal sense,' on its two different levels, can designate both that which must be given figurative interpretation because it is unedifying, and that which need not, or must not, be interpreted figuratively, because it is normative as it stands, or one might even say, because it is already spiritual. Furthermore, the unedifying literal sense, on the bottom level, is regarded as a *figura* or *signum*."

For readings of the *De doctrina* that simply identify spiritual with figurative interpretation see, e.g., Peter Szondi, "Introduction to Literary Hermeneutics," translated by Timothy Bahti, *New Literary History* 10 (1978): 17–29, esp. 21, and Tzveton Todorov, "The Birth of Occidental Semiotics," in *The Sign: Semiotics around the World*, edited by R. W. Bailey, L. Matejka, and P. Steiner (Ann Arbor, 1978), 1–42, esp. 36.

30. See Pamela Bright, *The Book of Rules of Tyconius: Its Purpose and Inner Logic* (Notre Dame, 1988), esp. 22–23; Karlfried Froehlich, ed., *Biblical Interpretation in the Early Church* (Philadelphia, 1984), 25–28; and Preus, *From Shadow to Promise*, 9–12.

even though the name of the particular trope employed is not found in the art of rhetoric (*in loquendi arte*), he uses a figurative expression (*tropica locutio*). [3.37.56]

On Augustine's testimony, then, both he and Tyconius would seem to agree that there are two distinct kinds of rules: the one is broadly legal and includes the equitable or spiritual interpretation; the other is broadly stylistic and covers all kinds of figurative statement, even those not actually treated in the *ars loquendi* or, more specifically, under elocution or style.

Augustine's insistence on the practical coincidence between the literal (*propria*) and the spiritual reading, moreover, recalls Cicero's defense of literal reading in the *De inventione* (2.44.128). Like Cicero's defender of *scriptum*, arguing that the *scriptor* intended to be interpreted according to his words, Augustine, too, prefers the literal meaning of the text to the private, unverifiable, hidden meaning discovered in the course of a misguided figurative interpretation; and Augustine's reading of particular passages of Scripture illustrates this preference.

Although it is possible, he concedes, to interpret Isaiah 58:7—*Et carnem tuam ne despexeris*—either literally (*proprie*), to mean one's body, or figuratively (*translate*), to mean all Christians born from the seed of the Word, "a collation of translations makes it probable that the meaning is a literal precept that we should not despise those of our own blood" (2.12.17). On the same principle, Augustine prefers Jerome's translation of Amos 7:14–15 to that of the Septuagint because on this occasion the inspired Seventy confound the spiritual with the figurative reading by rendering the original more figurative (*tropica*) and therefore more obscure (*obscuriora*) (4.7.15).[31] Augustine, moreover, associates this error with gentile, especially Greek, exegetical practices (3.6.10–3.9.13).

Whereas the Judaizing interpretation, as we have seen, fails to look beyond what is written to the writer's intention, the Hellenizing interpretation neglects *scriptum* altogether as the necessary foundation of exegesis, embracing in its place the useless proliferation of unintended figurations. "But just as it is a servile infirmity to follow the letter (*litteram sequi*) and

---

31. See 3.29.40 for Augustine's brief discussion of individual tropes, including *allegoria*, *aenigma*, and *parabola*. On the relation between *trope* and *figure*, see Quintilian 9.1.4.

to take signs for the things that they signify," Augustine warns, "in the same way it is an evil of wandering error to interpret signs in a useless way" (3.9.13). If the Jew, on Augustine's account, adheres inflexibly to only one side of the legal coupling of *scriptum* and *voluntas*, the Greek clings equally misguidedly to only one side of the stylistic pairing of literal and figurative signification. And if Jewish reading practices result in carnal servitude (*carnalis servitus*) (3.9.13), Greek reading practices, excessively figurative, obscure authorial intention behind a comparably carnal and servile veil (*servile carnaleque velamen*) (3.7.11). In contrast to both of these enslaving hermeneutics, Augustine advocates the *libertas spiritualis* of a Christian interpretation-theory (3.9.13, 3.8.12).[32]

By its own polemical account, then, the *De doctrina*'s way of reading is a middle way. Cautioned to avoid the extremes of Jewish legalism and Greek allegorism, Christian interpreters are encouraged in all cases to read

32. Augustine's characterization of Christian exegetical method as a mean between the Judaizing and Hellenizing extremes is anticipated by Diodore of Tarsus (d. before 394), whose hermeneutical works, known to both Basil and Augustine, establish a crucial distinction between *theōria* and *allēgoria*. Whereas *theōria*, like *dianoia* or *voluntas*, is derived from the literal or historical sense, *allēgoria* discards this sense altogether. Diodore describes the approved method as follows: "This method neither sets aside history nor repudiates *theōria*. Rather, as a realistic, middle-of-the-road approach which takes into account both history and theoria, it frees us, on the one hand, from a Hellenism which says one thing for another and introduces foreign subject matter; on the other hand, it does not yield to Judaism and choke us by forcing us to treat the literal reading of the text as the only one worthy of attention and honor, while not allowing the exploration of a higher sense beyond the letter also. In summary, this is what the person approaching the interpretation of the divine psalms ought to know" (Prologue to *Commentary on the Psalms*, translated by K. Froehlich in *Biblical Interpretation in the Early Church*, 86).

In the Preface to his Commentary on Psalm 118, Diodore also emphasizes the relation between interpretation and accommodation, a relation so central to the tradition I am tracing, but once again distinguishes the means of accommodation in the allegorical method from his own. Whereas the allegorizers "introduce foolish fables of their own making in place of the text," Diodore reads the words of the prophets as "adapted . . . both to the time in which they were speaking and to later times. Their words sounded hyperbolic in their contemporary setting but were entirely fitting and consistent at the time when the prophecies were fulfilled" (ibid., 91).

On Basil's familiarity with Diodore, see Richard Lim, "The Politics of Interpretation in Basil of Caesarea's *Hexaemeron*," *Vigiliae Christianae* 44 (1990): 351–70, esp. 354–59. And see H. N. Bate, "Some Technical Terms of Greek Exegesis," *Journal of Theological Studies* 24 (1923): 59–66, and Froehlich, *Biblical Interpretation in the Early Church*, 19–23.

spiritually—that is, charitably or equitably.[33] They are encouraged, in other words, to search out the author's intention by interpreting his words both according to his time, place, person, and so on and within Scripture as a whole. Thus historically and textually contextualized, the words of Scripture, Augustine affirms, reveal the divine willingness to read us even as we have read.

33. On the early Christian perception of the extremes of Judaism and Hellenism, see Jaroslav Pelikan, *The Christian Tradition: A History of the Development of Doctrine*, vol. 1 (Chicago, 1971), 11–67.

CHAPTER FOUR

Erasmian Hermeneutics
The Road to *sola scriptura*

I n the *Enchiridion* (1503), an early work designed to arm the Christian soul for the encounter with worldly experience, Erasmus recommends reading pagan literature as a propaedeutic for reading Scripture, not only handing on Basil's and Augustine's similar recommendations but even singling out these two favored Church Fathers as the esteemed authorities behind such a program. Like his favorites, moreover, Erasmus imagines reading the literature of pagan antiquity as an odyssey that threatens the unprepared reader with its pleasures:

> As a matter of fact, for the early stages of this campaigning I would not disapprove of the new recruit's getting some practice in the works of pagan poets and philosophers; only let him take them up in moderation, in a way appropriate to his immaturity and, so to speak, in passing—without expending his life on them and rotting, as it were, on the crags of the Sirens. To such studies as these Saint Basil calls the young men he educated in Christian character, and our Augustine called his friend Licentius back to the Muses. . . . Literature shapes and invigorates the youthful character and prepares one marvelously well for understanding Holy Scripture, to pounce upon which with unscrubbed hands and feet is something akin to sacrilege. Jerome chides the effrontery of those who, coming straight out of secular studies, dare to expound the Scriptures; but how much more

impudent is the behavior of those people who pre-
sume to do that very same thing without even a taste
of those disciplines.[1]

Inheriting the views of Basil and Augustine on the foundational role of
classical culture in Christian education, Erasmus also inherits their interpretive strategies for accommodating its literature to the circumstances of
his time.

Indeed, among the ancient disciplines most basic to the right
understanding of *scriptura* Erasmus numbers rhetoric and grammar, forg-
ing his hermeneutics, as we shall see, out of the rhetorical and grammatical tradition of interpretation that I have been tracing.[2]

1. *The Enchiridion of Erasmus,* translated by Raymond Himelick (Indianapolis, 1963), ch. 3, 50–51.

2. The influence of grammar and rhetoric on Erasmus's hermeneutics has been widely discussed. See, e.g., John William Aldridge, *The Hermeneutics of Erasmus* (Richmond, 1966); Jerry H. Bentley, *Humanists and Holy Writ: New Testament Scholarship in the Renaissance* (Princeton, 1983), 112–93; Marjorie O'Rourke Boyle, *Erasmus on Language and Method in Theology* (Toronto, 1977), and *Rhetoric and Reform: Erasmus' Civil Dispute with Luther* (Cambridge, Mass., 1983); Louis Bouyer, "Erasmus in Relation to the Medieval Biblical Tradition," in *The Cambridge History of the Bible,* vol. 2 (Cambridge, Mass., 1969), 492–505; Terence Cave, *The Cornucopian Text: Problems of Writing in the French Renaissance* (Oxford, 1977), 78–111; Jacques Chomarat, "Les *Annotations* de Valla, celles d'Erasme et la grammaire," *Histoire de l'exégèse au XVIe siècle* (Geneva, 1978), 202–28, "Grammar and Rhetoric in the Paraphrases of the Gospels by Erasmus," *Erasmus of Rotterdam Society Yearbook* 1 (1981): 30–68, and *Grammaire et rhétorique chez Erasme,* 2 vols. (Paris, 1981); Kathy Eden, "Rhetoric in the Hermeneutics of Erasmus' Later Works," *Erasmus of Rotterdam Society Yearbook* 11 (1991): 88–104, and "Equity and the Origins of Renaissance Historicism: The Case for Erasmus," *Yale Journal of Law and the Humanities* 5 (1993): 137–45; H. J. de Jonge, "*Novum testamentum a nobis versum:* The Essence of Erasmus' Edition of the New Testament," *Journal of Theological Studies* 35 (1984): 394–413; J. K. McConica, "Erasmus and the Grammar of Consent," *Scrinium Erasmianum,* vol. 2, edited by J. Coppens (Leiden, 1969), 77–99; John W. O'Malley, "Grammar and Rhetoric in the *pietas* of Erasmus," *Journal of Medieval and Renaissance Studies* 18 (1988): 81–98; "Erasmus and the History of Sacred Rhetoric: The *Ecclesiastes* of 1535," *Erasmus of Rotterdam Society Yearbook* 5 (1985): 1–29; John B. Payne, "Toward the Hermeneutics of Erasmus," *Scrinium Erasmianum,* vol. 2, edited by J. Coppens, (Leiden, 1969), 13–49; "Erasmus and Lefèvre d'Etaples as Interpreters of Paul," *Archiv für Reformationsgeschichte* 65 (1974): 54–83; Erika Rummel, "God and Solecism: Erasmus as a Literary Critic of the Bible," *Erasmus of Rotterdam Society Yearbook* 7 (1987): 54–72, *Erasmus' Annotations on the New Testament* (Toronto, 1986), and "St. Paul in Plain Latin: Erasmus' Philological Annotations on I Corinthians," *Classical and Modern Literature* 7 (1987): 309–18; Charles E. Trinkaus, "Erasmus, Augustine and the Nominalists," *Archiv für Reformationsgeschichte* 67 (1976): 5–32; and James Michael Weiss, "*Ecclesiastes* and Erasmus: The Mirror and the Image," *Archiv für Reformationsgeschichte* 65 (1974): 83–108.

Rooted in Ciceronian *interpretatio scripti,* this tradition, as we have seen, presupposes the accommodative function of all interpretation, not least in its two principal strategies: historical and textual contextualization. Whereas the interpretive principle of historical context finds its productive analogue in the rule of *decorum,* textual context, as a principle of reception, reverses, as it were, rhetorical *oeconomia;* and both productive principles serve the fundamentally rhetorical task of accommodating the speech to the demands of the particular occasion: its time, place, audience, speaker, and so on.

As we have also seen, equity, the ethical and legal counterpart to rhetorical accommodation, figures prominently in this tradition. In its efforts to negotiate between fixed legal statute and the infinite variety and particularity of human experience, equity institutionalizes the principles of intentionality and integrity or wholeness both in judging legal and ethical actions and in interpreting legal documents.

Squarely in this tradition, Erasmus confronts directly the accommodative nature of all interpretation. Building on Augustine's monumental Christian reconstruction of Ciceronian *interpretatio scripti,* Erasmian hermeneutics not only advances the spiritual reading of texts so central, as we have seen, to the interpretation-theory of the *De doctrina;* it also brings into sharp relief the affiliation of this right kind of Christian reading to the equitable interpretation of texts put forward by the rhetorical manuals of antiquity.[3] Erasmus, in other words, is a devoted student of ancient rhetoric, including its cardinal rule of *decorum,* whose interpretive counterpart, we recall, is historical context. Not surprisingly, then, he pursues

---

On the continued close relation into the sixteenth century between rhetoric and grammar, see, e.g., G. A. Padley, *Grammatical Theory in Western Europe, 1500–1700* (Cambridge, 1976), esp. 9: "It should however be noted that not only in Italy but throughout western Europe the sixteenth century offers many examples of grammatical treatises which continue to make a distinction between that *grammatica methodice et horistica* whose end is the establishment of normative rules, and the *grammatica exegetice sive enarrativa et historica* devoted to philological and rhetorical considerations. Everywhere, Renaissance grammar remains to a large extent bound up with rhetoric."

3. So according to J. K. McConica, *Erasmus* (Oxford, 1991), 14: "There is nothing mysterious about his educational masters: they are those of antiquity, Quintilian and Cicero among the foremost. Following thereupon, inevitably, is the *De doctrina christiana* of Augustine." See also his "Erasmus and the Grammar of Consent," 91.

this right kind of reading not only as a spiritual man—*homo spiritalis*—and an equitable interpreter—*interpres aequus*—but equally, as I shall argue, as a historicist.

The equation of spiritual, equitable, and historicist reading fundamental to Erasmian hermeneutics finds clear formulation, as we might expect, in his several treatises about biblical exegesis, including the *Methodus, Ratio, Ecclesiastes,* and *Annotations on the New Testament.* Before turning to these works, however, I wish to introduce the principles and strategies they advance in the context of Erasmus's controversial, even inflammatory, work in dialogue form on literary imitation, the *Ciceronianus* (1528). For the equation of spiritual, equitable, and historicist reading, as we shall see, finds an unmistakable analogue in spiritual, equitable, and decorous literary production, drawing our attention to, on one hand, the continued interaction for the humanists between rhetoric and hermeneutics and, on the other, to Cicero's formative role in the development of both.[4]

Deploying the cherished Ciceronian procedure of arguing on either side of the question (Lat. *disputatio in utramque partem*), the *Ciceronianus* stages a debate in the voices of its three interlocutors not over whether Cicero should be imitated but rather over how he should be imitated. The contest, in other words, brings face to face two opposed methods of literary imitation, both claiming the title of Ciceronian. The opposition between the two sides, moreover, is articulated by means of some of the very same legal and religious concepts whose conflation I examined in the hermeneutics of Augustine.

Speaking first and echoing the discredited position of Aristotle's *akribodikaios* (see above, 12–13), later associated by some Christians with Jews and Judaizers, Nosoponus advocates a rigid, legalistic, literal imitation of Cicero.[5] More zealous, by his own confession, in the pursuit of

4. On other similarities between the *Ciceronianus* and *Ecclesiastes,* see Weiss, "*Ecclesiastes* and Erasmus: The Mirror and the Image," 93–95.
5. In his essay "Erasmus's *Ciceronianus*: A Comical Colloquy," *Essays on the Works of Erasmus,* edited by Richard L. DeMolen (New Haven, 1978), 216, Emile V. Telle refers in passing to Nosoponus' Ciceronianism as "a religion . . . a superstition, a sort of literary Pharisaism." See also Hanna H. Gray, "Renaissance Humanism: The Pursuit of Eloquence," *Journal of the History of Ideas* 24 (1963): 497–514, esp. 513–14, and T. M. Greene, *The Light in Troy* (New Haven, 1982), 181–86.
Unless otherwise indicated, quotations in Latin from Erasmus's works refer either to

Ciceronianism than sainthood, he practices a devotion to his apostle, Cicero, that qualifies as idolatry (345–46). Surrounded by icons of the Roman orator, Nosoponus meditates continuously not on Scripture but on Cicero's extant works, learning them word for word and by heart.

Indeed, Nosoponus's affection for each and every word of Cicero motivates both his untiring labor on the *index verborum* (347), a list of words found in Cicero's writing, and his harsh judgment on even the slightest deviations from Ciceronian usage. A single slip, he insists, mars a whole composition, a standard applied without exception: "I make no exceptions. No one will be Ciceronian if even the tiniest word (*dictiuncula*) is found in his works which can't be pointed to in Cicero's *opus*. I shall judge a man's entire mode of expression (*totamque phrasim*) spurious and like counterfeit money if even a single word which doesn't bear Cicero's stamp finds a lodging there" (LB, 1:976D; 349). For Nosoponus, in other words, the judgment of the part determines the judgment of the whole—a legal code Bulephorus finds more severe than Draco's (LB, 1:976E; 350): "[A] whole book (*totum volumen*) is condemned for one little tiny word (*unam dictiunculam*) which isn't quite Ciceronian, when it's otherwise stylish and eloquent." As judge and critic, Nosoponus freely admits, he emulates the stern Areopagite (354).

Bulephorus, in stark contrast, elevates the whole above the part, rejecting the exact and meticulous (*superstitiosa*) imitation advanced by Nosoponus: "But just think what a lot is implied in a few words when one says 'the whole Cicero.' Yet, ye Muses above, what a tiny portion of Cicero is offered by those Ciceronian apes who scrape up a few phrases, idioms, figures, and rhythmical patterns from here and there and then exhibit just a top surface" (LB, 1:986A; 369, cf. 388, 446).[6] Exact in their use of Cicero-

---

Desiderii Erasmi Roterodami opera omnia, edited by J. Leclerc, 10 vols. (Leiden, 1703–6), cited hereafter as LB, or *Ausgewählte Werke*, edited by Hajo Holborn (Munich, 1933), cited hereafter as Holborn. For an English translation I have used *The Ciceronian*, translated by Betty I. Knott, in *The Collected Works of Erasmus*, (Toronto, 1986), vol. 28, hereafter cited as *CWE*.

6. On the traditional contrast in rhetorical theory between the meticulously labored composition and the more broadly conceived and roughly executed but more emotionally powerful speech, see Wesley Trimpi, "The Meaning of Horace's *Ut Pictura Poesis*," *Journal of the Warburg and Courtauld Institutes* 36 (1973): 1–34, and "Horace's 'Ut Pictura Poesis': The Argument for Stylistic Decorum," *Traditio* 34 (1978): 29–73.

nian *verba*, these literal Ciceronians fail to capture the mind or spirit—the *mens*—of their model (LB, 1:989C). Adapting the opposition between *mens* (or *voluntas*) and *verba* fundamental to Ciceronian *interpretatio scripti*, Bulephorus also adapts the strategy of the resurrected lawmaker so closely allied, as we saw in chapter 1, with the arguments for the priority of the intention of the *scriptor* over his *scriptum*.

Throughout his defense, in fact, Bulephorus relies on the hypothesis of a *Cicero redivivus* to make his point. If Cicero were alive today he would scarcely recognize, much less revere, the actual *words* transmitted in many cases erroneously by careless and ignorant scribes (363). On the contrary, Bulephorus insists, "[I]f he were alive now, he would say the same things as we do" (373, cf. 361, 381). In contrast to Nosoponus, then, Bulephorus advocates a method of imitation that upholds the whole over the part and the intention over the words, taking account of the variety and change-ability of circumstance. He advocates, in other words, a more equitable form of imitation. Recalling the earliest characterizations of equity in Aristotle's *Rhetoric* and *Ethics*, this method, again in contrast to Noso-ponus's, looks to accommodate exceptions (365). Its architectonic princi-ple, moreover, is *decorum*, whose alliance with equity, as we have seen, looks back to these same Aristotelian works and the rhetorical tradition they engender.

Although it takes into account the traditional variables of subject mat-ter, speaker, audience, place, and time (380, 383, 386, 396), Bulephorus's brand of *decorum* nevertheless foregrounds the last, and especially the inevitable changes in circumstance over time: "Well, the dress that suits a child is not appropriate to an old person; what is suitable for a woman would not be right for a man; the clothes for a wedding would not be proper for a funeral; and what was admired a hundred years ago wouldn't be acceptable now" (LB, 1:991C; 381).[7] Encouraged by the outspoken

---

7. On this historicist dimension of Erasmian *decorum*, see especially G. W. Pigman III, "Imitation and the Renaissance Sense of the Past: The Reception of Erasmus' *Ciceronianus*," *Journal of Medieval and Renaissance Studies* 9 (1979): 155–77.

    On the emerging historicism of the Renaissance, see, e.g., Donald R. Kelley, *Foundations of Modern Historical Scholarship* (New York, 1970), "Hermes, Clio, Themis: Historical Inter-pretation and Legal Hermeneutics," *Journal of Modern History* 55 (1983): 644–68, and "Civil Science in the Renaissance: The Problem of Interpretation," in *The Languages of Political Theory in Early-Modern Europe*, edited by A. Pagden (Cambridge, 1987), 57–78; and Zachary

agreement of not only his ally, Hypologus, but even his opponent, Nosoponus, on this last point, Bulephorus reasons that just as a resurrected
Apelles would not paint contemporary Germans as he had ancient Greeks
(381), so Cicero, if he were alive today, would write differently now than
he had then. Indeed, to imitate Cicero, whose genius lay in accommodating the particular occasion, is paradoxically to write in language that is
anything but Ciceronian taken precisely or literally. To write like Cicero
according to the letter, in other words, is to be unlike him in spirit: "It may
well be that the most Ciceronian person is the one least like Cicero, the
person, that is, who expresses himself in the best and most appropriate
way, even though he does so in a manner very different from Cicero's—
which would hardly be surprising, considering that everything has been
altered" (399). And whereas Nosoponus's precise imitation compels him to
choose between Ciceronianism and Christianity, Bulephorus's more equitable or spiritual imitation effectively reconciles the two. "There is nothing
to stop a person speaking in a manner that is both Christian and Ciceronian," he insists, "if you allow a person to be Ciceronian when he speaks
clearly, richly, forcefully, and appropriately, in keeping with the nature of
his subject and with the circumstances of the times and of the persons
involved" (400).

It is by promoting the historicism inherent in *decorum*, then, that Bulephorus fulfills his opening promise to plead both Cicero's case and his own
(*& Ciceronis, & nostram agi causam*) (LB, 1:981C; 360). For any method of
imitation based on ancient models, like any legal code regulated by fixed
statutes, must continue to reflect on the particular circumstances that in-
formed the original practices in order to assess the appropriateness of
those practices to new and often unforeseen circumstances. Such a method
must regard with equal discernment the past and the present, making the
necessary accommodations between them. Like so many lawyers trained in
Cicero's school, Bulephorus rests his case for the right kind of imitation on
a plea for equity.

Echoing his spokesman in the *Ciceronianus*, Erasmus, now in his her-

---

Sayre Schiffman, *On the Threshold of Modernity: Relativism in the French Renaissance* (Baltimore, 1991), and "Renaissance Historicism Reconsidered," *History and Theory* 24 (1985):
170–82.

meneutical works and in his own voice, calls for a method of interpretation that is similarly accommodative, not, however, after the fashion of the allegorizers.[8] For they freely exploit the accommodative power of allegory in their exegetical practices by utterly neglecting the historicity of the text they interpret: its belonging to another time and place. And here Erasmus has in mind not only the despised *neoterici* but even, in some instances, Origen, the most esteemed of the Greek Church Fathers (see, e.g., *Ecclesiastes*, LB, 5:1038E–1043B).[9]

At the other extreme, Erasmus also reproaches the so-called Judaizers,

8. On the role of accommodation in Erasmian interpretation, see especially Manfred Hoffman, "Erasmus on Language and Interpretation," *Moreana* 28 (1991): 3–20, and *Rhetoric and Theology: The Hermeneutic of Erasmus* (Toronto, 1994); and Eden, "Rhetoric in the Hermeneutics of Erasmus' Later Works," 88–104. On allegorical reading and writing as a form of accommodation, see, e.g., *Ratio*, Holborn, 261, 282, 284, and Hoffman, *Rhetoric and Theology*, 105–12, esp. 106: "The pivotal role which allegory plays in Erasmus' exegesis is analogous to the crucial place which accommodation obtains in his theology." Professor Hoffman and I disagree, I think, on how closely Erasmus identifies the allegorical with the spiritual meaning. In my understanding, Erasmus, like Augustine, leaves plenty of room for meanings that are at once non-figurative and spiritual.

For the relation between *commoditas* and *accommodatio* in Erasmus see Hoffman, *Rhetoric and Theology*, 178–83, and cf. the *commoda verba* of the "Letter to Dorp" (see above, 2).

On the accommodative nature of Christianity itself, see the *Paraclesis*: "This doctrine in an equal degree accommodates (*accommodat*) itself to all, lowers itself to the little ones, adjusts itself to their measure, nourishing them with milk, bearing, fostering, sustaining them, doing everything until we grow in Christ. Again, not only does it serve the lowliest, but it is also an object of wonder to those at the top. And the more you shall have progressed in its riches, the more you shall have withdrawn it from the shadow of the power of any other. It is a small affair to the little ones and more than the highest affair to the great. It casts aside no age, no sex, no fortune or position in life" (Holborn, 141–42; *Christian Humanism and the Reformation: Selected Writings of Erasmus*, translated by John C. Olin [New York, 1965], 96). See in addition Boyle, *Erasmus on Language and Method in Theology* 122–25; Chomarat, *Grammaire et rhétorique chez Erasme*, 1109–13; and John B. Payne, *Erasmus: His Theology of the Sacraments* (Richmond, 1970), 48–53.

For scriptural exegesis in humanism more generally, see Charles Trinkaus, *In Our Image and Likeness* (Chicago, 1970), 563–614. And see Salvatore I. Camporeale, *Lorenzo Valla: Umanesimo e Teologia* (Florence, 1972).

9. For Erasmus on allegory, see *Ratio*, Holborn, 278, 280, and *Ecclesiastes*, LB, 5:1010A–1051D. And see Boyle, *Erasmus on Language and Method in Theology*, 117ff.; Chomarat, *Grammaire et rhétorique chez Erasme*, 568–86; and Payne, "Toward the Hermeneutics of Erasmus," 35–49. See also Karlfried Froehlich, "Always to Keep the Literal Sense in Holy Scripture Means to Kill One's Soul: The State of Biblical Hermeneutics at the Beginning of the Fifteenth Century," *Literary Uses of Typology from the Latin Middle Ages to the Present*, edited by Earl Miner (Princeton, 1977), 20–48.

who just as thoroughly reject the role of figurative expression in Scripture, mistakenly identifying its meaning with the literal signification of the words (*E diverso, fuerunt qui sic oderunt tropos, ut universam Scripturam in eum sensum accipiendam putarint, quem ipsa verba simpliciter exprimunt,* LB, 5:1037D). Like Cicero's advocate of *scriptum* as characterized by his advocate of *voluntas,* these interpreters fail to look beyond the words to the writer's intention. Their commitment to the literal meaning, however, in no way fosters historical understanding, for they reject equally any attempt at historical reconstruction, a rejection justified on the grounds of a rigidly literal interpretation of Moses' words at Deuteronomy 4:2:

> Moreover, they [i.e., the Judaizers] distort what is
> written in Deuteronomy and Revelation—"Add
> nothing to my words and take nothing away"—to
> mean that it is wicked when editing the Old Testa-
> ment to consult the Hebrew sources or Greek transla-
> tions, or in the New Testament, to search from Greek
> codices either a better reading or a more original
> meaning (*sensum magis germanum*), although the
> scriptural passage in question means something
> entirely different; indeed, whoever compares passages
> and uses the ancient languages to establish the origi-
> nal meaning (*germanum sensum*) fulfills Moses' order.
> On the contrary, whoever from the words of Scrip-
> ture wrongly understood interprets one thing for
> something else, takes away not the words (*verba*) but,
> what is worse, the very intention (*ipsam mentem*) of
> Scripture, and substitutes what Scripture does not
> acknowledge. [LB, 5:1027F; my translation][10]

Rehearsing the lesson learned from the *De doctrina,* the openly acknowledged model for Erasmus's exegetical theory, he, like Augustine (see

---

10. For Erasmus's position on Judaism more generally, see Shimon Markish, *Erasmus and the Jews,* translated by Anthony Olcott (Chicago, 1986), and Heiko A. Oberman, "Three Sixteenth-Century Attitudes toward Judaism: Reuchlin, Erasmus and Luther," in Oberman *The Impact of the Reformation* (Grand Rapids, 1994), 81–121, esp. 102–6.

above, 61–63), qualifies the hermeneutics he advances as a *sobria medioc-ritas* (LB, 5:1043B), a middle ground between the allegorizing and Judaizing methods.[11] As characterized by the passage just quoted, this intermediate method looks to recover a *sensus magis germanus*, a meaning "more original" or "more familiar," taking "familiarity" in the Plutarchan or Basilian sense of *oikeios*—"at home."[12] And Erasmus identifies this *sensus germanus* not with the signification of Moses' words, or *verba*, but with his *mens*, or intention.[13]

If for Erasmus interpretation aims at understanding a meaning with which not only the reader but also the author would feel at home, the means of reaching this understanding include not only knowing languages and comparing translations, both mentioned above, but also locating passages in their historical and textual contexts. So Erasmus, like Cicero, Quintilian, and Augustine before him, recommends investigating those very circumstances of production covered under the rhetorical principle of *decorum:* speaker, audience, time, place, and so on (see, e.g., *Annotationes*, LB, 6:695F; *Methodus*, Holborn, 158; and *Ratio*, Holborn, 196–97, 285–86). And like these same predecessors, he instructs the exegete to explicate dif-

11. On similar extremes in the *Ciceronianus*, see LB, 1:1025C, *CWE*, 28:447. On the direct and pervasive influence of the *De doctrina*, see, e.g., *Ecclesiastes*, LB, 5:849BC, 1048EF, 1267F, 1290D, and Holborn, 150, 159, 178, 181, 184, 190; and see Charles Béné, *Erasme et Saint Augustin, ou l'influence de Saint Augustin sur l'humanisme d'Erasme* (Geneva, 1969), esp. 59–95, 142, 337, and Chomarat, *Grammaire et rhétorique*, 167–79.

12. Cf. LB, 5:1019AB, 1026A, and see Terence Cave, *The Cornucopian Text: Problems of Writing in the French Renaissance* (Oxford, 1979), 88–111. Cave emphasizes the innovation in Erasmus's choice of adjective for *sensus* and characterizes this qualifier as follows: "*Germanus* denotes close relationship, consanguinity, and a consequent affective reciprocity" (90). Its opposite, he reminds us, is *alienus* (89). The pair of opposites *germanus/alienus* corresponds, then, to the Greek *oikeios/allotrios*, so crucial to both Plutarch and Basil. Without explicitly using the language of *oikonomia*, in other words, Erasmus preserves its accommodative aspect in a Latin equivalent.

13. On Erasmus's preservation of the traditional distinction between signification and intentionality, see, e.g., *Contra morosos*, LB, 6:**4v. For this distinction in Renaissance hermeneutics, more generally, see Ian Maclean, *Interpretation and Meaning in the Renaissance: The Case of Law* (Cambridge, 1992). Maclean discusses briefly the role of ancient *interpretatio scripti* in Renaissance legal hermeneutics (75–86, 142–58). See also Maclean, "The Place of Interpretation: Montaigne and Humanist Jurists on Words, Intention and Meaning," in *Neo-Latin and the Vernacular in Renaissance France*, edited by Grahame Castor and Terence Cave (Oxford, 1984), 252–72.

ficult passages in light of what precedes them and what follows them. For Scripture often says obscurely in one place what it openly declares in another (e.g., *Ratio*, Holborn, 197; cf. *De doctrina* 2.9.14).[14] Furthermore, the meaning of any part of Scripture must accommodate the meaning of the whole:

> In the same way, to use Scripture properly it is not enough to isolate four or five little words (*quattuor aut quinque decerpsisse verbula*); rather one must investigate the sources of what is said. Frequently the meaning of a passage depends on what came before. It depends on who is speaking, to whom, when, on what occasion, with what words, and in what frame of mind; what precedes the passage in question and what follows it (*a quo dicatur, cui dicatur, quo tempore, qua occasione, quibus verbis, quo animo, quid praecesserit, quid consequatur*). Only in the context of these questions can what is meant be understood from what is said (*quid sibi velit quod dictum est*). In this matter, there is the further rule that the meaning which we elicit from obscure words respond to the whole of Christian doctrine (*ad orbem illum doctrinae Christianae*), to the whole of Christ's life (*ad illius vitam*), and finally to natural equity (*ad aequitatem naturalem*). . . . Here I should also mention the error of those who isolate from Scripture, in which diverse

---

14. For Erasmus on *collatio locorum*, see Hoffman, *Rhetoric and Theology*, 179–81.

Without mentioning explicitly Erasmus's debt to *interpretatio scripti*, Weiss offers the following characterization of Erasmus's hermeneutics in the third book of *Ecclesiastes:* "Furthermore, while he had rejected forensic rhetoric for homiletical uses, he applied some of its elements as hermeneutical tools: he derives his method of explaining Scripture in part from the methods of evaluating witnesses and legal documents proper to judicial oratory. These methods in turn incorporate the hypothetical and deductive methods used by other humanist rhetoricians to determine other historical possibilities. Thus the exegete might proceed by asking, how did the ancients interpret this passage? How do similar passages illumine this passage? How would the persons in this text probably have behaved? Might their customs explain their behavior? What proceeds and follows this passage *in situ*?" ("*Ecclesiastes* and Erasmus: The Mirror and the Image," 103).

things are narrated according to the diversity of
times, events, and peoples, those details that serve
their own desires, since no one understands human
law without understanding each and every chapter.
[*Ratio*, Holborn, 285–86; my translation]

Thoroughly in keeping with his attack on Folly's detractors in his "Letter
to Dorp" (see above, 1–3), Erasmus here condemns the interpretive
method that "plucks" (*decerpere*) a few words out of context, isolating the
part from the whole. On the contrary, as Erasmus illustrates by analogy
with the law, each and every biblical passage must be read in the context of
Scripture as a whole, including the whole of Christ's ministry and teaching. Only contextualized in this way—both historically and textually—
can what is meant be understood from what is said—the *voluntas* behind
the *scriptum* or *verba*.[15]

Inheriting from the rhetorical tradition of interpretation the opposition
between the words of *scriptura* and the intention of the *scriptor*, Erasmus
also inherits the alliance between the arguments for intention and equity,
arguments that Aristotle and Cicero, as we saw in chapter 1, had allied with
wholeness (see above, 18–19). So Erasmus presupposes, in the passage just
quoted, the congruence of the sacred text as a whole with Christ's life as a
whole and with equity.[16] Yet whenever an incongruity does arise between

15. See, e.g., Nancy Struever, *The Language of History in the Renaissance* (Princeton,
1970), esp. 74: "There is an important assumption about the past involved in this hermeneutic: i.e., that there is a coherence and integrity about the intention, about the experience of
either sacred or secular author behind the literary work which goes beyond, which tran-
scends, literal or conventional meaning. By means of his grammatical and rhetorical erudi-
tion the Humanist critic establishes the text as an integral, concrete experience in the past.
Thus the intention, the hidden saying is neither occult prophecy nor pagan wickedness; by
recovering the intention one recovers a completely comparable psychological experience of
objective historical value."

16. On the ancient origins of *aequitas naturalis*, see A. A. Schiller, *Roman Law* (The
Hague, 1978), 556–58. On the historical relation between equity and natural law, see Max
Hamburger, *The Awakening of Western Legal Thought*, translated by Bernard Miall (London,
1942), 125–27; for the place of this relation in Erasmus's philosophy, see Otto Schottenloher,
"Lex Naturae und Lex Christi bei Erasmus," in *Scrinium Erasmianum*, edited by Coppens,
2:253–99, and Hoffman, *Rhetoric and Theology*, 120–22.

For Erasmus's thinking about equity, see especially the adage *summum ius summa iniuria*,
LB, 2:374DE, *CWE*, 32:244–45. His reflection on this legal maxim ("extreme law is extreme

an interpretation of a particular passage and equity, Erasmus advises the interpreter to ask, in the words of a nearly contemporary English translation of his long annotation on 1 Corinthians 7:39 (c. 1550), "whether the rigor of this law, may any thing be mitigated, and loosed any manner of ways forsomuch as often times, such causes do come between, that it would appear a cruel thing not to help the party which is in danger" (LB, 6:695F).[17] Here as in the "Letter to Dorp," then, the equitable interpretation of words as well as deeds mitigates the harshness of an excessively literal construction.

Indeed, it is precisely in cases such as these that the biblical exegete, like the Roman orator, applies the strategies of historical and textual context:

> But if this law doth seem to be something repugnant
> to the equity of nature (*aequitate naturali*), we must
> see then, whether that which is written as concerning
> this law by the Evangelists and Apostles in their writings,
> may receive some other interpretation or meaning
> (*interpretanda sint*) than that, which is according
> to the open words of the law. And I would that it
> should be lawful for us to do in this case, as we are
> told to do in other places of the Scripture. And likewise,
> I would that we should discuss, and examine
> what times, to whom, and for what occasion (*quando,
> quibus, qua occasione*), it was spoken, and peradven-

---

injustice") signals the long-standing conflation of equity not only with the Roman tradition of natural law but with the Pauline reformulation of the unwritten law of the New Covenant engraved on the heart in opposition to that of the Old Covenant engraved in stone. See also Guido Kisch, *Erasmus und die Jurisprudenz seiner Zeit* (Basel, 1960), and Maclean, *Interpretation and Meaning in the Renaissance: The Case of Law,* 171–78.

17. *The censure and iudgement of the famous clark Erasmus of Roterodam: whyther dyvorcements betwene man and wyfe stondeth with the lawe of God, with divers causes wherfore it is permitted, with the mynde of the olde doctours, wrytten by the said Erasmus in the booke of his Annotations, upon these wordes of Paul, 1,cor,vii* . . . , translated by Nycolas Lesse (c.1550, University Microfilms FP38). For quotations in the text I have modernized the spelling. See E. J. Devereux, *Renaissance English Translations of Erasmus* (Toronto, 1983), 36–37. And see Guy Bedouelle, "The Consultations of the Universities and Scholars Concerning the 'Great Matter' of King Henry VIII," in *The Bible in the Sixteenth Century,* edited by David C. Steinmetz (Durham, 1990), 21–36.

ture, we shall find out the right understanding (*veram germanamque sententiam*) thereof [LB, 6:695F, trans. Nycolas Lesse].

Arguing once again for the sacred *scriptor*'s intention over his words— "right understanding" in this case translating the Latin *germana sententia* —Erasmus, like his teachers in the ancient rhetorical tradition, complements these strategies with that of the resurrected lawmaker. Surely if Paul, master-rhetorician and advocate of accommodation, were alive today, he would interpret his own words equitably, taking account of changing circumstances and human weakness: "If such cases (I say) were put to Paul, peradventure considering the circumstances of the case (*causae circumstantiis*), he would make some other answer than he hath made, he would somewhat release the rigor and straightness (*de rigore*) of his former counsel, and peradventure would otherwise also and more gently (*civilius*) interpret, and understand his writings than we do" (LB, 6:701E, trans. Lesse).[18] Like the *Cicero redivivus* of the *Ciceronianus*, who teaches us how to write, the Paul of the *Annotations* teaches us how to read.

Faced with the differences between first-century Corinth and sixteenth-century Europe, Erasmus argues, Paul, in keeping with his efforts to interpret his own words equitably, interprets these same words historically, with an eye to the particularities, including time, place, and so on, that determined them. For it is only through such a historical reconstruction that the interpreter comes to understand not so much what the words themselves mean but what the writer meant and thus how that writer would accommodate his meaning to new and unforeseen circumstances. Like rhetorical

18. On Paul's commitment to accommodating his audience see, e.g., *Ratio*, Holborn, 196; *Ecclesiastes*, LB, 5:1065EF, and "Letter to Paul Volz," (1518), *CWE*, 6:82: "Paul makes many concessions to the Corinthians, distinguishing for the time being what ideal he would set before those who are perfect in the Lord's name and what indulgences he would allow to the weaker brethren in his own name; but always in the hope that they may make progress. Over the Galatians he broods a second time until Christ take shape in them." For the comparable accommodations of Moses and Jesus, according to Erasmus, see, e.g., *Paraphrasis in Marcum*, LB, 7:233AF, *CWE*, 49:121–23, and my "Equity and the Origins of Renaissance Historicism: The Case for Erasmus." See also Robert D. Sider, "Concedo nulli: Erasmus' Motto and the Figure of Paul in the Paraphrases," *Erasmus in English* 14 (1985–86), 7–10.

imitation, then, biblical hermeneutics as both practiced and preached by Erasmus is an act of accommodation, one in which both writer and reader come to feel at home. Like Bulephorus, his spokesman in the *Ciceronianus,* Erasmus, in his own voice in his mature hermeneutical works, pleads a double case: both Paul's and his own.

CHAPTER FIVE

A Rhetoric for the Reader

Melanchthon's *Elementorum rhetorices*

The Erasmian brief for an alliance between rhetorical imitation and biblical hermeneutics finds its most compelling advocate in Philip Melanchthon, whose impact on educational theory and practice in northern Europe from the early sixteenth to the late eighteenth centuries is second only to that of Erasmus. Indeed, Melanchthon's singularly influential *Elementorum rhetorices duo libri* (1531), the last word of the so-called *praeceptor Germaniae* on the art of rhetoric, sets in sharpest relief this humanist's insights into the complementarity between composition and interpretation, between rhetorical production and literary reception.[1] For his handbook on the elements of rhetoric in two books, the first covering invention and disposition and the second elocution, provides nothing less than a rhetoric for the reader, and especially the reader of *scriptura*. Whereas Erasmus, as noted in chapter 4, articulates a theory of imitation in the *Ciceronianus* coincidental with his theory of interpretation in, for instance, the *Methodus* and *Ratio*, Melanchthon not

---

1. For Melanchthon's influence as the *praeceptor Germaniae*, see Helmut Schanze, "Problems and Trends in the History of German Rhetoric to 1500," *Renaissance Eloquence: Studies in the Theory and Practice of Renaissance Rhetoric*, edited by James J. Murphy (Berkeley, 1983), 108–9, 120–25; and John W. O'Malley, "Content and Rhetorical Forms in Sixteenth-Century Treatises on Preaching," in *Renaissance Eloquence*, edited by Murphy, 241–46.

The *Elementorum rhetorices duo libri* is the last of three manuals, following the *De rhetorica* (1519) and the *Institutiones rhetoricae* (1521). See Ralph Keen, *A Checklist of Melanchthon Imprints through 1560* (St. Louis, 1988), 50–54. Shortly after publication, the *Elementorum* was adapted into English by Leonard Cox. See his *The Art or Crafte of Rhetoryke* (1532), edited by Frederic Ives Carpenter (Chicago, 1899). See also John Monfasani, "Humanism and Rhetoric," in *Renaissance Humanism: Foundations, Forms, and Legacy*, vol. 3, edited by Albert Rabil, Jr. (Philadelphia, 1988), 200–201, and Hans-Georg Gadamer, "Rhetorik und Hermeneutik," in *Gesammelte Werke*, vol. 2 (Tübingen, 1986), 282–91.

only integrates his instructions concerning the two activities of skillful reading and writing into a single work but teaches one set of rules for both practices. As we shall see, in fact, his rhetoric addresses the reader more than the writer, working alongside his *Loci communes* (1521) to provide a complete hermeneutics.[2] Geared, like Plutarch's *De audiendis* and Basil's *De adolescentes*, to an audience of young students, the *Elements* begins with a straightforward statement of its aim: to "prepare young people (*adolescentes*), not so much for speaking correctly (*ad recte dicendum*), but for prudently evaluating and understanding the writings of others (*ad prudenter intelligenda aliena scripta*)" (76–77).[3] Even those who may never themselves compose discourses, forensic or theological, need an art or method (*via, ratio*) of understanding and judging such writing, especially insofar as it generates controversy (76).

Stressing throughout his art the points of comparison between legal and theological controversy (cf. 114, 139, 151, 219), Melanchthon also rehearses the analogy fundamental to this tradition—a tradition shared once again with Plutarch and Basil—between reading and journeying. Just as writers must check their use of foreign or wandering words—*peregrina vocabula*—to avoid becoming obscure and thus losing their audience,

2. On the *Loci communes theologici*, see *Melanchthon and Bucer*, edited by Wilhelm Pauck, *The Library of Christian Classics*, vol. 19 (Philadelphia, 1969), 9–17; Quirinus Breen, "The Terms 'Loci Communes' and 'Loci' in Melanchthon," in *Christianity and Humanism: Studies in the History of Ideas* (Grand Rapids, 1968), 93–105; Robert Kolb, "Teaching the Text: The Commonplace Method in Sixteenth-Century Lutheran Biblical Commentary," *Bibliothèque d'Humanisme et Renaissance* 49 (1987): 571–85; Zachary Sayre Schiffman, *On the Threshold of Modernity: Relativism in the French Renaissance* (Baltimore, 1991), 11–18; and John Schneider, *Philip Melanchthon's Rhetorical Construal of Biblical Authority: Oratio Sacra* (Lewiston, N.Y., 1990), 205–62.

For Erasmus's suggestion, subsequently taken up by Melanchthon, that the exegete discover and organize *loci theologici*, see *Methodus*, in *Ausgewählte Werke*, edited by Hajo Holborn (Munich, 1933), cited hereafter as Holborn, 158–59, and *Ratio*, edited by Holborn, 291. And see Wilhelm Maurer, *Der Junge Melanchthon*, vol. 1 (Göttingen, 1967), 171–214, and Schneider, *Philip Melanchthon's Rhetorical Construal of Biblical Authority*, 68, 108.

3. For text and translation I have used, and where necessary modified, Sister Mary Joan La Fontaine, "A Critical Translation of Philip Melanchthon's *Elementorum Rhetorices Libri Duo*" (Ph.D. diss., University of Michigan, 1968). See also *Corpus Reformatorum* (hereafter *CR*), vol. 13, edited by Charles G. Bretschneider (Halle, 1846), 412–506; and see Werner Alexander, *Hermeneutica Generalis: Zur Konzeption und Entwicklung der allgemeinen Verstehenslehre im 17. und 18. Jahrhundert* (Stuttgart, 1993), 135–41.

so readers without a method for resolving obscurities, and especially for seeing through an estranging complexity to its more familiar underlying order and arrangement, "[become] lost like strangers in an unknown country (*velut hospites in ignota regione errabant*), if they [happen] at any time to come upon [Paul's] disputations" (205). These same interpreters of Paul (*interpretes Pauli*), Melanchthon claims earlier in book 1, failing to see how a variety of arguments fits under one heading or topic (*ad unum aliquod caput accommodanda*), "wander whole worlds away from [Paul's] real meaning (*toto coelo a sententia aberrabant*)" (116).[4]

Like Erasmus, moreover, Melanchthon associates interpreting Paul with imitating Cicero. Recalling the *Ciceronianus,* the *Elements* ends with an extended treatment of imitation (301–42), and more precisely *imitatio Ciceronis*. And like Bulephorus in the Erasmian dialogue, Melanchthon argues for a spiritual rather than a literal imitation, one that captures not the *verba* but what Melanchthon calls the *hexis,* the mind-set of Cicero (318). Characteristic of that mind-set in the *Elements,* recalling the *Ciceronianus,* is the commitment not only to following several models but to deviating from those models when *decorum* requires it (303, 306, 319, 336).[5] Equally characteristic is a commitment to the whole of Ciceronian discourse over its individual parts—not isolated words (*singula verba*) but the totality and integrity of Ciceronian style (*phrasis*) and arrangement (*collocatio*) (319). Even when Cicero borrowed bits and pieces from Greek philosophers and historians, Melanchthon insists, he integrated them into writing that was entirely his own: "The arrangement and the entire body of the speech represent Cicero" (*Collocatio enim et universum corpus orationis Ciceronem referebat*)" (320).[6]

---

4. Not incidentally Melanchthon demonstrates the literalizing method of reading practiced by the Jews with their interpretation of the scriptural passages promising return home: "There is a great subject of contention with the Jews on the written word. They imagine that the kingdom of Christ is of this world, that is, that when they have received their homeland (*patria*), they are going to reign in Jerusalem" (161).

5. Like Bulephorus, Melanchthon argues specifically for the decorum of non-Ciceronian words accommodating non-Ciceronian circumstances, especially those related to Christianity: "The imitator will not reject words of course even though non-Ciceronian if the case requires them such as in theological controversies the name of Christ, of Church, *fides* for *fiducia* and similar terms should be used" (319). See also *Scholia in Ciceronis de oratore Librum II, CR,* 16:722–27.

6. Like Erasmus in his letter to Dorp, Melanchthon rejects not only the writers but also

Melanchthon's treatment of imitation in book 2, and in particular his emphasis on *dispositio* or arrangement—Cicero's skillfully integrated *collocatio*—supplements his brief discussion of disposition at the end of book 1. Not surprisingly, in view of the tradition we have been tracing in the previous chapters, Melanchthon there refers to the guiding principle of organization or arrangement as *oikonomia*, a principle as crucial to literary interpretation as to literary composition:

> And this, namely the οἰκονομία, is to be considered
> when we have to read the speeches of learned per-
> sons, not only in order that we may understand the
> writings of others (*aliena scripta*) more correctly, but
> also in order that we may be able to see in our own
> affairs what will be most valuable where, which mat-
> ters belong in the introduction, which ones seem to
> be most useful, as it were, in the first line of battle,
> which ones are harmful, and best hidden somewhere
> in the middle. These rules cannot be handed down in
> an "art (of Rhetoric")" since nobody is able to include
> all occasions and affairs. [206–7][7]

Like the Greek and Roman educators he most admires, especially Quintilian (see above, 27–31), Melanchthon reinforces at once the centrality of *oikonomia* to the arts of rhetoric and hermeneutics and its resistance to the hard and fast rules of these arts. Indeed, *oikonomia* in matters of arrange-

---

readers who pluck (*decerpunt*) isolated words and passages from here and there: "And because they proclaim that the accumulation of notable sayings is the perfect learning, they have no other purpose in reading the writings except to pick (*decerpant*) from them just like flowers certain sayings (*dicta*). In the meanwhile, they learn no art perfectly, they do not understand any writing in its entirety, and they consider nowhere the entire character of rhetoric" (194). On those who regard the part over the whole in composition, see also 319.

7. On the need to understand the arrangement of Paul's letters in order to understand their meaning, see 204. Melanchthon also opens book 2 with a reference to Xenophon's *Oeconomia* and the need for good organization (*ordo*), here *taxis* (217), especially in *oratio*.

For the poet's use of *oeconomia*, see *Enarratio comoediarum Terentii, CR,* vol. 19, edited by H. E. Bindseil (Brunsveig, 1853), 703, 706, 724, and *Declamatio de praefatione in Homerum, CR,* 11:406–7, citing both Horace and Quintilian on the *mos Homericus*. And see above, 28–29.

ment, as counterpart to decorum in matters of style and equity in matters of law, represents the flexible, qualitative measure, like the rule of soft lead of Aristotle's lesbian builders, designed to accommodate, in a way generalized rules never can, the particular circumstances of individual cases. This accommodation in turn favors the whole over the part—the overall effect of the discourse being produced and the entire set of circumstances it seeks to represent: not the part, in Aristotle's familiar characterization of equity (see above, 19), but the whole, not who the defendant is at this very moment, but what kind of person he has been always or for the most part.[8]

This privileging of wholeness in matters of *dispositio* or arrangement, epitomized by the principle of *oikonomia*, corresponds to the concept of *status* in Melanchthon's treatment of invention. Central to the tradition beginning with the hellenistic rhetorical treatise of Hermagoras (see above, 13), this concept forms the very core of not only Melanchthon's rhetorical but also his hermeneutical theory. For both the reader and the writer must begin by locating the *status* of the discourse in question:

> No part of the art (of rhetoric) is more necessary than the precepts dealing with the status of the case (*de statibus*), in respect of which, this is first and foremost: in relation to every problem (*negocio*) or controversial question (*controversia*) we consider what the status is, that is, what is the chief subject of inquiry (*principalis*

8. For Melanchthon as commentator of Aristotle's *Nicomachean Ethics* (with book 5 appearing first in 1532), see *CR*, 16:399–411, and *A Melanchthon Reader,* translated by Ralph Keen (New York, 1988), 179–201; and for his *Epitome ethices* (also 1532), and especially his discussion of equity, or *epieikeia,* see *Philosophiae moralis epitome, CR,* 16:74–77, and *A Melanchthon Reader,* 224–26: "Epikeia is mitigation of the laws in some circumstance that does not conflict with justice. For it does not condone crimes but punishes them more mildly on account of some circumstance. . . . Further, epikeia reveals itself most clearly in all interpretations of laws. For there is no law which can be observed with equal severity in all cases without epikeia. Thus an interpretation must be applied to all laws which directs them to more humane and lighter sentence. . . . Thus equity is ruled by some superior law so that it may preserve the superior laws; so Christ violated the sabbath and touched lepers against the laws. . . . Finally the gospel itself is a certain epikeia of divine law, since it approves of those who do rightly even if they do not satisfy the law." In addition, Melanchthon delivered at least two declamations on this topic: *De aequitate et iure stricto* (1542) and *De stricto iure et aequitate* (1544), *CR,* 11:551–55, 669–75. Cf. Hans-Georg Gadamer, *Truth and Method,* translated by Joel Weinsheimer and Donald G. Marshall (New York, 1989), 318.

quaestio), the proposition that contains the gist of the matter (*summam negocii*) toward which all arguments are aimed, in other words, the main conclusion. No matter of debate can be comprehended, nothing can be explained, stated or grasped in an orderly fashion, except some proposition be formulated which includes the sum total of the case (*summam causae*). [115][9]

Status, then, is introduced as the proposition containing the *summa negocii* or *summa causae*, what we might call "the heart of the matter." Elaborating on Ciceronian terminology (*De inventione*, 1.4.5), Melanchthon also refers to this single most important element of discourse, its *summa*, as its *finis*, *intentio*, *voluntas*, and *scopus* (93–94). Alongside grammarians practicing *enarratio poetarum* and rhetoricians practicing *interpretatio scripti*, those same interpreters of Paul mentioned above succeed or fail depending on whether in reading Paul they can locate the *status* of his discourse and its resident *summa*, *voluntas*, or *scopus* (116).[10]

9. See also 116: "[S]tudents are to be assiduously made accustomed in reading speeches and disputations of eloquent speakers to seek out the status of the case, to establish propositions in (their own) writing and speaking and fit their arguments to these." And see Schneider, *Philip Melanchthon's Rhetorical Construal of Biblical Authority*, 78–86, 239; Monfasani, "Humanism and Rhetoric," 200–201; and John O. Ward, "Renaissance Commentators on Ciceronian Rhetoric," *Renaissance Eloquence*, edited by J. J. Murphy (Berkeley, 1983), 171–73.

10. On *scopus* (Gr. *skopos*) as a technical term of exegesis, or *enarratio*, especially among neoplatonists, see James Coulter, *The Literary Microcosm: Theories of Interpretation of the Later Neoplatonists* (Leiden, 1976), 77–94, Malcolm Heath, *Unity in Greek Poetics* (Oxford, 1989), 124ff.; Robert Lamberton, "The Neoplatonists and the Spiritualization of Homer," in *Homer's Ancient Readers: The Hermeneutics of Greek Epic's Earliest Exegetes*, edited by Robert Lamberton and John J. Keaney (Princeton, 1992), 116–17; and Frances Young, "The Rhetorical Schools and Their Influence on Patristic Exegesis," *The Making of Orthodoxy: Essays in Honor of Henry Chadwick*, edited by Rowan Williams (Cambridge, 1989), 182–99, esp. 191. On its use by grammarians, see Martin Irvine, *The Making of Textual Culture: 'Grammatica' and Literary Theory, 350–1100* (Cambridge, 1994), 126, quoting Donatus concerning Virgil's *Eclogues*: "The purpose (*intentio*) of the book, which the Greeks call *skopos* [aim, end], is established in imitation of the poet Theocritus, who was Sicilian and Syracusian. The purpose is also to praise Caesar and other leaders, through whom he had his home and lands restored; whence the effect and end of the poem produce delight and usefulness according to precepts." For Erasmus's use of *scopus*, see, e.g., *Methodus*, Holborn, 156, where it is closely associated with *summa*, and "Letter to Paul Volz," *CWE*, 6:79–81; Margaret O'Rourke Boyle, *Erasmus on Language and Method in Theology* (Toronto, 1977), 74ff.; and Hoffman, *Rhetoric*

The interpretive failures Melanchthon compares to Horace's failed poetry, compared, in turn, to failed painting and pottery, all artistic productions that in the execution fall short of the artist's intention, often by forfeiting an integrity that Horace himself refers to as *summa operis* (*Ars Poetica* l. 34; cf. *Elements,* 115–16, and *Ars Poetica* ll. 1–9, 21–22).[11] Just as the rhetorical model of literary production concentrates on the *intentio* or *summa* resident in the *status* of the case, so the rhetorical model of literary reception or hermeneutics demands the same concentration in the act of reading. Antithetical to this model is the one associated with the *neoterici:* "For some have foolishly taught (*tradiderunt*) that there are four ways of interpreting Scripture: the literal, tropological, allegorical and anagogical. And without distinction every verse of the entire Scripture has been expounded in four ways. However it can easily be shown how faulty this is. For a speech becomes confused (*incerta*), divided into so many meanings (*discerpta in tot sententias*)" (242). While the *neoterici* read to proliferate *sententiae,* or meanings, thus rendering the text more uncertain, Melanchthon, by his own characterization, reads for the *summa* or *intentio* of the discourse accessible through its *status.*[12]

---

and Theology: The Hermeneutic of Erasmus (Toronto, 1994), 41ff. On the distinction between Melanchthon's and Erasmus's use of *scopus,* see Schneider, *Philip Melanchthon's Rhetorical Construal of Biblical Authority,* 94, n. 156.

For Melanchthon's understanding of Paul's Letter to the Romans as the *scopus* of all *scriptura,* see Schneider, *Philip Melanchthon's Rhetorical Construal of Biblical Authority,* 130–42, and for his reading Roman comedy this way, see *Enarratio comoediarum Terentii, CR,* 19:731.

Like these other terms, *summa* is also a technical term of exegesis in this tradition. On the relation between *summatim* and *verbatim,* where the former is identical to *sententialiter*—the meaning as opposed to the words—in the medieval exegetical tradition, see Mary J. Carruthers, *The Book of Memory: A Study of Memory in Medieval Culture* (Cambridge, 1990), 89–90.

Just as the interpreter must read for the *summa* or *scopus,* the writer, as part of invention, must move from the hypothesis to the thesis: "But we shall add to the rules on invention a single one, since it has the greatest force in all disputations, that is that we have to convert the hypothesis into the thesis" (*Elements,* 189). For Christ's special ability as orator to perform this conversion, see 192.

11. On the frequent comparison in this manual between literature and painting, also an aspect of the argument in the *Ciceronianus,* see 89, 220, 343; Noel L. Brann, "Humanism and Germany," in *Renaissance Humanism,* edited by Rabil, 2:148; and D. B. Kuspit, "Melanchthon and Dürer: The Search for the Simple Style," *Journal of Medieval and Renaissance Studies* 3 (1973): 177–202.

12. See also *Elementorum rhetorices, CR,* 13:466, on the allegorizers, those *ineptissimi, qui in sacris litteris omnia transformant in allegorias.* And on Augustine's interpretive theory and

Having thus introduced *status*-theory into all reading and writing—and thus taking for granted the paradigmatic nature of legal discourse—Melanchthon rehearses the division of cases based on the division of *status* into its traditional three kinds: (1) the conjectural status, answering to whether or not a deed was done (*an sit*), (2) the legal status, answering to what was done (*quid sit*), and (3) the juridical status, answering to what kind of deed it was (*quale sit*); not its definition, which falls under the legal *status*, but its quality (115–68).[13]

Indeed, Melanchthon numbers definition (*definitio*) as the first of six grounds of controversy under the legal status (150) and one especially important not only to forensic but also to theological debate. To prove his point, he adduces the contemporary controversy over the Lord's Supper, a controversy fueled by opposing definitions of the term *sacrificia* (151).[14] The other five grounds of controversy, familiar to us from chapter 1, are contrary laws (*contrariae leges*), the discrepancy between the written word and the writer's intention (*scriptum et sententia*), ambiguity (*ambiguitas*), reasoning from analogy (*ratiocinatio*), and transference (*translatio*). Although he preserves the most inclusive list from the *Ad Herennium* (1.11.19–1.13.23), Melanchthon nevertheless follows Cicero and Quintilian in delineating the relation between the various grounds, meanwhile drawing our attention to the continuous role of rhetorical *interpretatio scripti* in hermeneutics, and especially in biblical hermeneutics.

---

practice as a necessary correction of Origen's *perniciosae interpretationes*, see *Declamatio de vita Augustini, CR*, 11:453–54.

For Erasmus on the reading methods of the *neoterici*, see above, 71.

13. For the role of the *status qualitatis* in the *status*-system, see Wesley Trimpi, *Muses of One Mind: The Literary Analysis of Experience and Its Continuity* (Princeton, 1983), 245–344. For Melanchthon on the *status qualitatis* and Quintilian, see *Elements*, 138.

14. See, e.g., *Responsio Philip. Melanth. ad quaestionem de controversia Heidelbergensi* (1559), *CR*, 9:961–63, translated by Lowell C. Green, *Melanchthon in English* (St. Louis, 1982), 25–28, esp. 25–26, where Melanchthon argues like a *grammaticus*: "And there is need to speak copiously about the benefit of the Supper in order that people may be stimulated in their love for this seal and in its frequent use. Also the word, koinonia, must be made clear.

Paul does not say that the nature of the bread is changed, as the papists say. He does not say, like the men at Bremen, that the bread is the substantial body of Christ. He does not say, like Hesshusius that bread is the true body of Christ. But he says it is the koinonia, that is, the thing by which it becomes consociated with the body of Christ. This takes place in the use, and not without thought, as when mice chew the bread."

For interpreters of *scriptura* often find themselves struggling to clarify obscurities. And their clarifications just as often engender debate not unlike that of the forum: "Very frequently in public (*in foro*) and Church affairs (*in Ecclesiis*) there are questions for debate on a written passage and its meaning (*scripti et voluntatis*), due to the ambiguity or the lack of clarity (*obscuritate*) of a piece of writing. The Greeks call this the status of what is said and its interpretation (ῥητοῦ καὶ διανοίας)" (158). Like Cicero and Quintilian, who also looks back to the Greek terminology (see above, 11), Melanchthon gives most attention to controversy grounded in the discrepancy between *scriptum* and *voluntas* (or *sententia*).

Cicero, we recall, provided the rhetorician in training with strategies for countering the advocates of *scriptum*. As we have also seen, Augustine and Erasmus later identify these same literalists with a Judaizing method of interpretation. Melanchthon, in contrast, associates the advocates of *scriptum* not only with the Jews but with the Anabaptists, who, while claiming, in contradistinction to the Jews, that all of Scripture is obscure, nevertheless argue strictly for *verba* and will admit no *interpretatio* (159).[15] So, Melanchthon claims, the Anabaptists practice a hermeneutics decried as fraud by legal experts insofar as it elevates the written word above the writer's intention. Roundly condemning such a hermeneutics, Melanchthon insists that discrepancies between *scriptum* and *voluntas*, frequently indicated by absurdity or obscurity in a passage, should be resolved by *dialectica*, or in other words, by proof (159).

Melanchthon, then, also preserves the rhetorical tradition of interpretation we have been tracing by safeguarding the distinction between the two most pervasive grounds of controversy: the discrepancy between the written word and the writer's intention and ambiguity. This distinction, we recall, marked in turn a corresponding division in the rhetorical art from its earliest manuals between matters of proof, treated under *inventio*, and matters of style, treated under *elocutio* (see above, 10–12). Whereas the ground of controversy called *scriptum et voluntas* (or *sententia*) is resolved for the most part by dialectic or proof, ambiguity, Melanchthon explains

---

15. For Melanchthon against the Anabaptists, see *A Melanchthon Reader:* "Refutation of Servetus and the Anabaptists' Errors," 169–77, "The Augsburg Confession," 97–125, and "On Philosophy," 65–70, esp. 68, where Melanchthon faults the Anabaptists, in addition to their doctrinal heresies, for being both unrefined in literature and unsuited to it.

(163), is most often decided *ex grammatica,* from forms and figures of speech (*phrasi et figuris*).

One effective proof for resolving the discrepancy between *scriptum* and *voluntas* is the application of the circumstances or *circumstantiae:* "There is, however, a general precept widely followed in this class of disputes that circumstances be examined, for from these we often hunt down the meaning (*sententiam*), and decide whether the written ordinance and its intention (*utrum scriptum et voluntas*) agree or disagree. And, indeed, the words of Hilary are true: Circumstances clarify rules (*dicta*)" (162). Among these circumstances Melanchthon includes the traditional seven (132), answering the questions who, what, where, by whose help, why, how, and when (*quis, quid, ubi, quibus auxiliis, cur, quomodo, quando*).[16] And he complements this strategy with another, equally effective in resolving the obscurity or absurdity arising from discrepancies between words and intentions: the comparison of the obscure or absurd passages with those whose meaning is evident (160), a practice often referred to in this tradition as *collatio locorum* (see above, 55–56).[17] Melanchthon, in other words, advises his young exegetes in training to seek to discover what an author means, as distinct from what his words say—his *voluntas* and not his mere *scriptum*—by taking the fullest possible account of historical and textual contexts.

As a manual for the writer, then, the *Elements* advocates a method of literary production based on Ciceronian imitation—not the narrowly construed *imitatio* of the strict Ciceronians but the broader, more equitable program first set forth by Cicero's most influential admirer, Quintilian and later by Bulephorus in the *Ciceronianus.* Equally central to Melanchthon's program, as we have seen, is the *status*-theory so amply treated by these same rhetoricians.

16. In the *Elements,* the *circumstantiae* also serve as a *locus communis* for establishing *facultas* in the conjectural status (131), for establishing rhetorical *color* (287–88), and for amplification (299). For the relation of the circumstances to history, see Schneider, *Philip Melanchthon's Rhetorical Construal of Biblical Authority,* 77, who quotes Melanchthon: "Two things are necessary for historical narration, circumstances and *loci communes.*"

For Erasmus on the relation between the circumstances and *status,* including references to Horace's *Ars,* in a way that recalls Melanchthon's treatment, see *Ecclesiastes* (1535), book 2, ASD V–4, 270–71, 344; and see Hoffman, *Rhetoric and Theology,* 162–67.

17. On the traditional complementarity between *circumstantiae* and *collatio locorum,* among English interpreters as well as German, see below, 103.

As a manual for the reader, the *Elements* also relies on Cicero and Quintilian, and not only on their *status*-theory but on their treatments of *interpretatio scripti* as well (see above, 7–19). Indeed, Melanchthon's hermeneutics can be said to find its spiritual center at the intersection of these two traditional rhetorical elements. For both *status*-theory and *interpretatio scripti* characterize matters in terms of controversy. Both insist on the priority of *voluntas*, what Melanchthon, borrowing from the grammatical tradition, also calls the *scopus* and *intentio;* and both provide strategies for resolving controversy, even overlapping strategies, such as the circumstances. Given the same training as Melanchthon's writer, Melanchthon's reader applies the strategies he has learned to *aliena scripta*, what someone else has written, in order to apprehend its meaning.

Converging so completely in Melanchthon's *Elements*, the histories of the rhetorical models of reading and writing eventually diverge. Subsequent centuries, as we well know, will outspokenly reject any method of literary production based on imitation, Ciceronian or otherwise. Meanwhile Protestant hermeneutics will fully absorb the humanists' rhetorical model of literary reception before struggling to free itself, in the words of one of its most illustrious theorists, from "the limits of the rhetorical viewpoint."[18]

---

18. Wilhelm Dilthey, "The Rise of Hermeneutics," translated by Frederic Jameson, *New Literary History* 3 (1972): 239. For Melanchthon's influence on Schleiermacher, see Schneider, *Philip Melanchthon's Rhetorical Construal of Biblical Authority*, 210–11.

CHAPTER SIX

Protestant Hermeneutics
Flacius's *Clavis scripturae sacrae*

T he *Clavis scripturae sacrae* (1567) of Matthias Flacius Illyricus, now almost unknown and virtually unread, enjoyed a very different fate not only in its own time but for centuries after. In addition to being reprinted numerous times during its first 150 years, it is singled out by the well-known Catholic apologist Richard Simon in his widely circulated *Histoire critique du Vieux Testament* (1678). According to Simon, the *Clavis* is an especially useful and learned tool for scriptural interpretation, in spite of the limitations of its Protestant polemics.

More recently, in his brief reconstruction of the early history of hermeneutics (1900), Wilhelm Dilthey accords Flacius's work special prominence. He labels it the first important and most profound hermeneutical work of the new learning associated with Renaissance humanism and draws special attention to its innovative techniques:

> If the exegete comes up against difficulties in his text,
> he overcomes them by referring to the context pro-
> vided by the actual lived experience of Christianity. If
> we now translate this concept out of its dogmatic mode
> of thought into our own, the hermeneutic value of
> religious experience becomes an individual instance
> of a more general principle, according to which every
> interpretive procedure contains as a factor exegesis
> from the objective [*sachlichen*] context. Alongside this
> religious principle of interpretation there exist other,
> more properly rational ones. The first of these is

grammatical interpretation. But besides this, Flacius understands the meaning of a psychological or technical principle of interpretation as well, according to which individual passages are to be interpreted in the light of the intent and form of the whole. And for the first time, applying this technical principle, he methodically draws on rhetorical judgment as to the inner coherence of a literary work, its form, and its most effective elements. The reworking of Aristotelian rhetoric by Melanchthon preceded him in this. Flacius is fully conscious of having thus applied, for the sake of an unambiguous determination of individual passages, a criterion inherent in the work's context, its purpose, its proportion, and in the coherence of its separate parts.[1]

This characterization of Flacius's contribution, including its deference to Melanchthon, illustrates not only the constant presence of Schleiermacher in Dilthey's reconstruction of the early history of hermeneutics but, more to the point here, the extent to which Flacius, contrary to Dilthey's assessment, actually forges his exegetical theory out of the principles of the rhetorical and grammatical tradition of interpretation we have traced thus far.[2] Like his predecessors in this tradition, Flacius takes for granted the

1. Wilhelm Dilthey, "The Rise of Hermeneutics," translated by Fredric Jameson, *New Literary History* 3 (1972): 238–39, and *Gesammelte Schriften*, vol. 2 (Leipzig, 1942), 117–25. See also Rudolf A. Makkreel, *Dilthey: Philosopher of the Human Studies* (Princeton, 1975), 259–60, and Georgia Warnke, *Gadamer, Hermeneutics, Tradition and Reason* (Cambridge, 1987), 5.

Following Dilthey, Gadamer names Flacius the founder of Protestant hermeneutics specifically and the first to conceive the task of hermeneutics more generally. See Hans-Georg Gadamer, *The Relevance of the Beautiful and Other Essays*, translated by Nicholas Walker (Cambridge, 1986), 149. See also *Truth and Method*, translated by Joel Weinsheimer and Donald G. Marshall (New York, 1989), 175.

On Flacius, see Jean Grondin, *Introduction to Philosophical Hermeneutics*, translated by Joel Weinsheimer (New Haven, 1994), 42–44; Barbara Kiefer Lewalski, *Protestant Poetics and the Seventeenth-Century Religious Lyric* (Princeton, 1979), 81–82; Rudolf Pfeiffer, *History of Classical Scholarship from 1300 to 1850* (Oxford, 1976), 93; and Debora Shuger, "Morris Croll, Flacius Illyricus, and the Origin of Anti-Ciceronianism," *Rhetorica* 3 (1985): 269–84, and *The Renaissance Bible: Scholarship, Sacrifice, and Subjectivity* (Berkeley, 1994), esp. 11–53.

2. Although it is a subject for another study, the influence of ancient hermeneutics on

complementarity between intentionality and signification as sources of meaning; and like his predecessors, he recommends the strategies of historical and textual context, including the decisive relation between the whole and the parts, for apprehending this meaning.

Insofar as Flacius looks ahead, then, he does so by looking back. Struggling to advance his own polemical ends, he lays the ground for the work of his Protestant successors, including Schleiermacher and Dilthey, by continuing the humanist enterprise of restoring the hermeneutics of antiquity.[3] While this hermeneutics is grounded in both rhetoric and its propaedeutic, grammar, Flacius makes a special effort, as Melanchthon before him, to return to the rules of *interpretatio scripti* as introduced by Cicero and preserved by Quintilian. As we have also seen, Augustine paves the way for this enterprise in his *De doctrina* by accommodating these same rules to Christian needs.[4] Indeed, Augustine even anticipates the metaphor

---

Schleiermacher is apparent throughout his writings. See especially *"The Hermeneutics:* Outline of the 1819 Lectures," translated by Jan Wojcik and Roland Haas, *New Literary History* 10 (1978): 1–16, where he establishes the relation of the parts to the whole and the distinction between two kinds of meaning and two kinds of context.

3. For Flacius's polemical activity, see Dražen Budiša, "Humanism in Croatia," translated by Ivo Banac in *Renaissance Humanism: Foundations, Forms, and Legacy,* vol. 2, edited by Albert Rabil, Jr. (Philadelphia, 1988), 286–87, and Dilthey, "The Rise of Hermeneutics," 237–40. See also Lewis Spitz, "Humanism and the Protestant Reformation," in *Renaissance Humanism,* 3:380–411.

For Flacius's association with Melanchthon at Wittenberg, first as student and then as colleague, see Budiša, "Humanism in Croatia," 286; *A Melanchthon Reader,* translated by Ralph Keen (New York, 1988), 14–16; and Oliver K. Olson, *Shapers of Religious Tradition in Germany, Switzerland, and Poland, 1560–1600* (New Haven, 1981), 1–17.

4. In focusing on the role of *interpretatio scripti,* I am unable to do justice to the corresponding continuity within the grammatical tradition from the Alexandrian exegetical principle of *Homēron ex Homērou saphēnizein* to the Reformers' *sola scriptura* or *scriptura sui ipsius interpres.* For Flacius on this principle, see, e.g., 2.20: "At contra, Scripturam dubiam, aut obscuram, per Scripturam exponere & dijudicare, tutissimum simul & utilissimum est; ita ut Deus ipse, ac eius verbum, sit omnium controversiarum, ac dubiorum, supremus iudex & diremptor."

On this matter Dilthey has an intriguing footnote that, briefly describing the two books of the *Clavis,* compares it to an instrument for interpreting Homer, a *clavis Homerica:* "Der erste Abschnitt ist eine treffliche lateinische Konkordanz. Der zweite umfasst Antiquitaeten, Kritik, Einleitung, was man biblische Rhetorik nannte, und Grammatik, miteinander verschmolzen. Man kennt ja das bunte Durcheinander solcher Werke in der damaligen Zeit, wie z. B. in der clavis Homerica" (*Gesammelte Schriften,* 2:117, n. 1).

On the Alexandrian principle, see Christoph Schaeublin, "Homerum ex Homero,"

behind Flacius's title, comparing the rules for exegesis to *claves,* keys for unlocking the meaning of the obscure passages of Scripture (*De doctrina* 3.30.42).[5]

Both the first book of the *Clavis,* a dictionary of biblical terms and expressions, and the second, a comprehensive treatment in several tracts of general principles governing interpretation, look to resolve scriptural obscurity, to elucidate the original, historical—in the etymological sense, radical—meaning of *scriptura:* what Flacius calls the *nativus sensus* and Erasmus had called, as we have seen (72–73), the *germanus sensus.*[6] Following both the *De doctrina* and the tradition of rhetorical *interpretatio scripti* that informs the *De doctrina,* the *Clavis* assumes three principal causes of obscurity: (1) a discrepancy between the writer's words and her or his intention, (2) ambiguity, and (3) contradiction.

Like his classical and early Christian sources, moreover, Flacius fully realizes that in many cases these grounds of controversy overlap and that in practice ambiguity, for instance, often gives rise to contradiction.[7] And

---

Museum Helveticum 34 (1977): 221–27; Pfeiffer, *History of Classical Scholarship from the Beginnings to the End of the Hellenistic Age,* 230–31, and James I. Porter, "Hermeneutic Lines and Circles: Aristarchus and Crates on the Exegesis of Homer," *Homer's Ancient Readers: The Hermeneutics of Greek Epic's Earliest Exegetes,* edited by Robert Lamberton and John J. Keaney (Princeton, 1992), 67–114.

On *sola scriptura,* see, e.g., Gerhard Ebeling, *The Word of God and Tradition,* translated by S. H. Hooke (London, 1968), 102–47, and Gerald L. Bruns, *Hermeneutics Ancient and Modern* (New Haven, 1992), 139–58.

5. For Erasmus on the key to understanding scripture, see, e.g., *Desiderii Erasmi Roterodami opera omnia,* edited by J. Leclerc, 10 vols. (Leiden, 1703–6), cited hereafter as LB, 6:599B (*Quandoquidem haec est velut una clavis ad intelligentiam Pauli, si quis animadvertat mutationem personarum, de quibus & ad quas loquitur*), and Jacques Chomarat, *Grammaire et rhétorique chez Erasme* (Paris, 1981), 1:583–84.

6. For Flacius on the need in all studies to return to the origin or source, see *Clavis Scripturae Sacrae seu De Sermone sacrarum literarum* (Jena, 1674), 2.36: "Illud est in omnibus scriptis ac studiis primarium, & quasi palmarium praeceptum: ut singulae materiae ac institutiones, ex suis praecipuis sedibus, aut fontibius, petantur & hauriantur." See also Quintilian 8.3.36.

Thanks are due to Seth Kasten and Drew Kadel, the librarians of the Rare Book Room of the Union Theological Seminary, for making this text readily available to me. Unless otherwise indicated, all quotations are from the second tract of the second book and all translations of Flacius are my own.

7. *Clavis Scripturae Sacrae* 2.41: "Sexto, ambiguitas sermonis valde multas contradictiones parit: ubi in altera contradictoriarum, eaedem voces aliter accipiuntur, quam in altera; quarum innumera sunt exempla."

like his sources—here he singles out Quintilian on contradictory laws—
Flacius takes for granted that resolving contradictions elucidates the words
that in turn preserve the writer's intention: "At this point [the exegete] does
what Quintilian advises: if we have diligently examined the law, we should
be able to find something in the words themselves (*in ipsis verbis*) that
resolve the contradiction and show the intention (*mentem*) of the legislator
to be otherwise" (2.40).[8] The ultimate aim of interpretation, in other
words, is to establish authorial intention, the *mens authoris:* to look beyond
the meaning or signification of the words to what the writer meant (*magis
in mentem, quam in verba Scriptoris, respicere*) (2.31).

As we have seen, this distinction between two kinds of meaning, intention and signification, pervades the rhetorical and grammatical traditions
of interpretation, often in the shorthand opposition between *mens* and
verba or *scriptum* and *voluntas*. And this opposition, as we have also seen,
not only forms the very foundation of ancient interpretation-theory as
revived by Melanchthon but also much early Christian, most especially
Augustinian, hermeneutics, with its double opposition between spiritual
and literal (*literalis, corporalis*) interpretation, on one hand, and figurative
(*translata, figurata*) and literal (*propria*), on the other. Flacius's hermeneutics clearly belongs to this tradition, reinforcing with its straightforward
exposition of terms the earlier transformation of rhetorical *voluntas* into
Christian *spiritus:* and this exposition clarifies, in turn, the affiliation, as we
saw in Erasmian hermeneutics, between equitable and spiritual reading.

Whether interpreting the word of God, prophet, apostle, or evangelist,
Flacius writes, the listener must attend to his *spiritus*. "By *spiritus*," Flacius
continues, "I mean the *ratio, mens, consilium* or *propositum* of the speaker.
Even if someone understands not only what, but why and even how; even
if someone understands the words (*verba*) or the sense (*sensum*) of the
speech (*orationis*), he understands little. Many fail in this way, but espe-

---

8. Cf. 2.39, where the strategies of *interpretatio scripti* are openly applied to *scriptura:*
"There are absolutely no real contradictions in Scripture (just as Quintilian says concerning
the laws): rather when they seem to disagree, we must consider it the fault of our own ignorance; we don't understand either the subject matter or the language; or we haven't suffi-
ciently considered the circumstances."
   See also 2.36, 116, and 117 on the *mens authoris*. For Quintilian on preserving the distinction between the three grounds of controversy, see 7.10.1–4, and above, 9–10.

cially the blind Jews, who cling to the letter. Consequently, they understand hardly at all the *spiritus* of the most important passages of Scripture" (2.82). For Flacius, as for Erasmus and Melanchthon, the meaning of Scripture resides ultimately in the intention, or *mens*, of the *scriptor*. Any interpretation that stops short at *scriptum*, at the *verba* themselves, without looking beyond to *voluntas* or *mens*, is literal in the sense of corporeal—an interpretation after the manner of the Jews.

The principal task of the interpreter, then, is to resolve obscurity, and this is accomplished only when, overcoming ambiguities and contradictions, the interpreter comes to understand the speaker's or writer's *voluntas* or *spiritus*. But if the aim or end of interpretation looks back to the rhetorical tradition of *interpretatio scripti*, so do the means; and these, too, as we have seen, are both institutionalized by the Roman rhetoricians, including Cicero and Quintilian, and appropriated for Christian needs by Augustine in the *De doctrina*.

Cicero, we recall, advises the orator to support his argument for an interpretation of some controversial document on the grounds of both evidence from the text (*scriptura*) itself—not only in its parts but as a whole —and from the author's life and works (see *De inventione* 2.40.117 and above, 17–19). Augustine follows Cicero in this advice, recommending that the exegete understand as fully as possible not only the *praecedentia* and *consequentia* of the passage in question but also the circumstances of its production, including the natural and human history that informs it (*De doctrina* 2.28.42–44, 3.4.8).

Inheriting the profound and enduring alliance between history and hermeneutics (cf. 2.11), Flacius also inherits the complementary concepts of historical and textual context. Unlike Cicero, Augustine, and even Erasmus, however, he refers to these concepts with a fully stable specialized terminology. Opposed, like most of his Lutheran cohort, including Melanchthon, to multiple, allegorical, hidden meanings in Scripture, he advocates a sound and simple *sententia* confirmed by both context (*cum perpetuo contextu*) and circumstance (*cum circumstantiis negotii*) (2.70).

Judging the investigation of *circumstantiae* among the most effective means of resolving obscurity, Flacius numbers them at six, including person, time, manner, cause, place, and instrument, and treats each in detail.[9] His detailed treatment, moreover, sets in relief their rhetorical origins. Under the consideration of *persona*, for instance, Flacius takes account of the usual rhetorical triad: speaker, subject, where the subject is a person, and audience, including both immediate and intermediate—divine and human—addressees.[10] Seeming to anticipate later hermeneutical reflection, he considers the second circumstance, time, preeminent insofar as both divinity and humanity accommodate it.[11] By qualifying *modus*, the third circumstance, as either fitting or unfitting—*conveniens* or *inconveniens*—and surrounding it with verbs such as *decere* and *accommodare*, he clarifies its association with the first rule of rhetorical composition, namely decorum (2.34; cf. Quintilian 5.10.52). And his treatment of *causa*, synonymous, as he claims, with *consilium*, *propositum*, and, notably, *voluntas*, recalls the overlapping list of synonyms in the definition of *spiritus*, quoted earlier: "In the fourth place among the circumstances, we have numbered *causa* or *consilium*, on which, for the most part action depends. Closely related to this is *affectus animi*, *intentio*, and *voluntas*, about which it is truly said that *voluntas* and *propositum* determine the quality of the deed" (2.34). Like action in general, the act of writing demands interpretation in light of the writer's intention. And for Flacius, as for Cicero, Augustine, Erasmus, and Melanchthon, this intention in turn becomes apprehensible in the light of historical circumstance.

Understood as the elaboration of the *circumstantiae* informing a text, historical context constitutes for Flacius one of the two most effective means of understanding *scripta* remote from the interpreter (*remotissima a nostra*) because of material (*ob res*) and linguistic conditions (*ob sermonem . . . a nostro more loquendi nimium alienum*) (2.31). The other is the estab-

9. "Circumstantiae plurimum faciunt, ad judicandum, cognoscendumque verum obscuri loci sensum. Eae autem sunt numero sex: Persona, tempus, modus, causa vel consilium, locus, & instrumentum de quibus singulis ordine dicam" (2.31).

Cf. 2.39, where a consideration of circumstances resolves contradictions; 2.5, where *conditio* is a synonym for *circumstantia;* and 2.117, where the *circumstantiae* are listed as *quis, quid, ubi, quoties, cur, quomodo, quando.*

10. At 2.32, Flacius lists *quae loquuntur; ad quam sit sermo; de qua; & denique etiam coram qua.*

11. "Secunda circumstantia est Tempus; quae & ipsa maximi momenti est. Nam non tantum humana in tempore geruntur, & ad tempora accommodantur; sed & Deus, alio tempore aliter, in quibusdam, cum hominibus egit" (2.33).

lishment of a textual context. Here again, Flacius not only follows the lead of his sources in antiquity, both classical and Christian, but once more explicates their principles with unprecedented clarity.

Cicero, we recall, advises the orator to examine a problematic passage not only in light of other passages in the same text, especially those that precede and follow the passage in question, but also as part of the text as a whole. Following the Ciceronian tradition of *interpretatio scripti,* Augustine emphasizes throughout the *De doctrina* both the usefulness of comparing passages—*collatio locorum*—and the explication of more obscure passages with the help of those that are clearer. Following this same tradition, Flacius gives *collatio locorum* second place only to the power of *Spiritus Dei* in illuminating the meaning of Scripture and cites Augustine as his source for the principle of interpreting whatever is obscure in the light of what is clear—*sic alius alium illustrabit* (2.7).[12] These *praecedentia, consequentia,* and other passages adduced for comparison constitute one aspect of textual context or what Flacius calls simply *contextus:* namely, the formal relation of part to part. Like Cicero and Augustine, but in much greater detail, Flacius also considers in his treatment of context the relation of part to whole.

As Dilthey claims above, consideration of the relation of part to whole occupies a key place in Flacius's hermeneutics. The text (*textus*), he stresses repeatedly, resembles the human body in its coherence and harmony: each part or member not only complements the other parts but also functions as part of a larger unity (2.13, 22, 53). While recalling the paradigmatic passage in the *Phaedrus* (264C) on the "organic" nature of rhetorical composition, Flacius delves beneath the Platonic metaphor to its more radical assumptions about unity and multiplicity, sameness and difference, quoting another Platonic commonplace to advance his argument for the formal integrity of *Scriptura:* "The many, in turn, even the most diverse, sometimes somehow come together to form one unified thing. Here, then, is that most useful lesson of Plato, *eph'hen kai polla horan:* to be able to discern

---

12. Cf. 2.15: "In expositione autem Scripturae, ac in eruendo eius vero sensu, maximam vim efficaciamque habet, post Spiritum Dei, collatio locorum Scripturae: qui vel verbis aut phrasi, vel etiam rebus, similes sunt. Sic etiam collatio partium unius loci; examinatio accurata praecedentium & consequentium: ut ipse contextus nobis obscuram sententiam illustret." See also 2.36, 37, 40.

and examine the one in the many and the many in the one" (2.13).[13] Like the human body, in other words, both *scriptum* in general and the more specialized *scriptura* are simultaneously a composite of individual parts—or passages—and a whole. In unifying the multiplicity (i.e., in making one of many), however, the whole represents something more than the aggregation of its parts.

Applying Plato's lesson of the one and the many directly to the formal property of rhetorical composition or discourse, Flacius surpasses his predecessors, ancient and even humanist, in clarifying the "circular" relation between textual unity and diversity: the whole text in relation to its parts.[14] In its hermeneutical application, as we have seen, this circularity finds its place in Flacius's treatment of context. But the wholeness or integrity of *scriptura*, like *scriptum*, is for Flacius, as for his predecessors, not only a formal property of discourse; it is also a logical property, complementing the relation of part to whole with that of particularity to generality or universality.

In the *De doctrina*, as we have seen, this logical relation between the general sense of the whole and the localized meaning of an individual passage underlies the much discussed canon of *caritas*, which Augustine identifies as the *summa* of Scripture (see above, 57). And it is this *summa*—what Melanchthon would also call the *finis*, *intentio*, or *voluntas*—that determines whether a passage should be interpreted literally or figuratively (1.36.40, 3.10.15, 3.15.23).

In the *Clavis*, Flacius not only reaffirms this relation, asserting the harmony between problematic passages of Scripture and the so-called *articolae fidei* (2.12), but he identifies this relation with another technical term, one closely related to *contextus* and already familiar to us from Melanchthon: *scopus*.[15] Together with the context, in fact, the *scopus* pro-

---

13. On the fundamental relation of unity and multiplicity in Plato's treatment of *logos*, see Hans-Georg Gadamer, "Plato's Unwritten Dialectic," in *Dialogue and Dialectic*, translated by P. Christopher Smith (New Haven, 1980), 124–55. On seeing one in many and many in one in *Phaedrus*, see, e.g., 263BC, 265D, and especially 266B.

14. For Flacius on circularity in style, especially Paul's, see 2.433–34, and Shuger, "Morris Croll, Flacius Illyricus, and the Origin of Anti-Ciceronianism," 276. And see Gadamer, *Truth and Method*, 175–77.

15. See Gadamer, "Rhetorik und Hermeneutik," in *Gesammelte Werke*, vol. 2 (Tübingen, 1986), 282–91, and above, 84.

vides the interpreter with his or her best instruments for understanding individual passages (*ut sensus locorum, tum ex scopo scripti aut textus, tum & ex toto contextu, petentur*) (2.26).

Using the same metaphor of the body, Flacius claims that all good writing (*sanum scriptum*) exhibits a *scopus*, likened in one place to the *genus* of the body and in another to its head and face. Like Melanchthon, he also calls the *scopus* the *finis* and the *intentio*—the overall purpose or intention of the text, which is carried out or fulfilled by the details.[16] Not incidentally, the *scopus* of the text shares with the *voluntas* of the author the concept of *intentio*, setting in relief not only the assumed complementarity of the logical and psychological aspects of meaning but their inevitable conflation. As the later tradition so amply demonstrates, the *intentio* or *scopus* of *scriptum* fuses with the *intentio* or *voluntas* of the *scriptor*.[17]

Although it inadvertently encroaches on the psychology of the author, however, the notion of *scopus*, for Flacius, accommodates more specifically the psychology of the reader, who, by nature, must grasp the text as a whole before understanding its individual parts. "It is a great benefit to the reader," Flacius claims, therefore, "if at the very beginning of his reading, there is some anticipation (*praemonitum*) of the *scopus* of the text and of the *genus* of *doctrina* and *materia* to be treated" (2.10). Indeed throughout the *Clavis*, Flacius insists that the psychology of the reader bears decisively

16. See especially the following two passages: "Cum igitur aggrederis lectionem alicuius libri; id statim initio, quoad eius fieri potest, age: ut primum scopum, finem, aut intentionem totius eius scripti, quod veluti caput aut facies eius est, protinus vereque notum habeas, qui pleraque paucis verbis notari potest. & non raro in ipso statim titulo notatur: sive is unus est, cum totum scriptum in unum corpus conformatum est, sive plures, cum sunt plures eius partes, prorsus inter se-se non cohaerentes" (2.22); and "Impossibile enim est, esse aliquod sanum scriptum, quod non certum scopum, certum quodam genus alicuius (ut ita dicamus) corporis, exhibeat; & aliquas partes aut membra in se complectatur, quae certo ordine, ratione, ac q. proportione, tum inter se, tum etiam cum toto corpore, ac praesertim cum scopo suo, sunt coagmentata" (2.23). Cf. 2.26.

17. This conflation is perhaps already evident in the term *sententia* and its corresponding genre. See G. Paré, A. Brunet, and P. Tremblay, *La Renaissance du XIIe siècle* (Paris, 1933), 267: "Ainsi *sententia* ne signifie-t-il pas directement l'opinion ou l'avis que l'auteur avait dans l'esprit, mais, par métonymie, la proposition même en laquelle s'exprime cette opinion. Témoignage du caractère impersonnel que, inévitablement, prend la sententia en passant de main en main, de recueil en recueil; c'est la 'sententia verborum' et son contenu qui vaut, non pas directement la 'sententia animi', la façon de penser de tel qui un jour l'exprima."

on his or her interpretation and that experience—*experientia*—is one especially decisive factor.[18]

Like so much of Flacius's hermeneutics, the reverence for experience looks back not only to Luther (see above, 4) but to the rhetorical tradition, where it forms one of the regular triumvirate of forces, with natural talent and art, ensuring oratorical success.[19] In keeping with the rhetorical tradition of interpretation that we have been tracing, Flacius transforms this crucial principle of production into a principle of reception, voicing in the preface to the second book special concern for the *lector imperitus*, the inexperienced reader.

In keeping with this concern, as we have seen, the second book of the *Clavis* both establishes a specialized vocabulary and recommends interpretive strategies to guide such a reader. But while reading, for Flacius, is an activity that can be illuminated by theory, it can be enlivened only by the experience that comes through practice. Indeed, interpretation for Flacius, as for this tradition more generally, is a *praxis*. Grounded in action, like the ancient arts of rhetoric and ethics, it is rooted in the particularities of the individual case. And individual cases demand individual judgments. With experience, then, Flacius's *lector imperitus* may aspire to become Erasmus's *interpres aequus*. Characterized in the "Letter to Dorp" and throughout the previous chapters, this equitable interpreter reads the part in the context of the whole and always in the light of historical circumstance. Such a reader, according to the advocates of this rhetorical tradition of interpretation, reaches beyond the words to the intention, beyond the letter to the spirit.

---

18. "Sextum remedium est hic quoque, sicut & in omnibus aliis scientibus ac artibus vera ac viva experientia; quae omnino obscuriora Theorices mirifice illustrat, ac declarat" (2.7). See also 2.94, 104.

For the status of experience, both as *Erlebnis* and *Erfahrung*, in hermeneutics, see Gadamer, *Truth and Method*, 60–70, 346–62.

19. See, e.g., *De oratore* 1.2.5, 1.32.145, and Quintilian 2.18.5–2.19.3.

Conclusion

Therefore I do not much like the opinion of the man
who thought by a multiplicity of laws to bridle the
authority of judges, cutting up their meat for them.
He did not realize that there is as much freedom and
latitude in the interpretation of laws as in their creation (*à l'interprétation des loix qu'à leur façon*). And
those people must be jesting who think they can
diminish and stop our disputes by recalling us to the
express words of the Bible. For our mind finds the
field no less spacious in registering the meaning of
others than in presenting its own. As if there were
less animosity and bitterness in commenting than in
inventing (*à gloser qu'à inventer*)![1]

In the sixteenth century's most compelling defense of experience, and
especially of experience grounded in reading, Montaigne places in evidence the very tradition of interpretation outlined in the foregoing chapters. It is a tradition, he confirms albeit epigrammatically, originating not
only in *interpretatio scripti*, the interpretation of laws, but even more in the
equitable interpretation of these laws. Against his nameless opponent, an
advocate of complexity in the legal code,[2] Montaigne rehearses the argument introduced by Aristotle and repeated by Cicero and Quintilian for

1. Montaigne, "Of Experience," in *Oeuvres complètes*, edited by Albert Thibaudet and
Maurice Rat (Paris, 1962), 1042; *The Complete Essays of Montaigne*, translated by Donald M.
Frame (Stanford, 1943; rpt. 1971), 815, cited hereafter as Frame.
2. Maurice Rat identifies "celuy-là" as Justinian (*Oeuvres complètes*, 1669), but it is possible that this opponent is as anonymous as "ceux là" of the sentence that follows.

the limited number and greater universality and simplicity of the laws.[3] For it is the task of the judge as the living interpreter of the lawmaker's intentions to accommodate the infinite variety and variability of human circumstances to a fixed and generalized set of rules. In making his case, Montaigne also reminds us of the adversarial nature of interpretation, and not only of legal interpretation but of biblical interpretation. Indeed, the juxtaposition of his two indictments in the passage quoted above, the first against the misguided advocate of many and complex laws, the second against those naively thinking to adjudicate theological controversy merely by invoking the words of *scriptura*, sets in high relief the development that I have charted from Cicero and Quintilian to Melanchthon and Flacius. As we have seen, in this tradition readers of legal *scripta* as well as *scriptura* aspire to reach beyond *scriptum* to *voluntas*, beyond *letter* to *spirit*, beyond words to meaning. And there is as much individuality and variety in the reception of the meaning of others as there is in the production of one's own. Or in Montaigne's terms, as much in the interpretation of the laws as in their creation: in glossing as in inventing. This is one distinctive feature that rhetoric and hermeneutics hold very much in common.

Side by side, then, Montaigne's pointed accusations of these unnamed adversaries—accusations made in the service of a larger defense of experience—provide a striking record of the profound interaction between rhetoric and hermeneutics in this tradition, and especially between writing and reading. As theorized in the sixteenth century, as we have seen, both of these activities seek authorization in Cicero. Toward the end of the century, moreover, Montaigne is free to reject not only *imitatio Ciceronis* but even its counterpart, *lectio Ciceronis*. For by his own account, Montaigne learns more from reading himself than from reading this other (*Oeuvres*, 1051; Frame, 821–22). If reading in this tradition is figured as the journey home, Montaigne has arguably laid claim to the most direct route.

---

3. On the famous Roman legal maxim *summum ius summa iniuria*, see Cicero *De officiis* 1.10.33, and Johannes Stroux, *Summum ius summa iniuria, ein Kapitel aus der Geschichte der interpretatio iuris* (Basel, 1926). For Erasmus's adage on this maxim, see above, 75, and see Melanchthon, *Philosophiae Moralis Epitome*, esp. the chapter entitled "Quid interest inter summum ius et ἐπιεικεία," in *Corpus Reformatorum* (hereafter *CR*), vol. 16, edited by Henricus Ernestus Bindseil (Leipzig, 1850), 73–78.

In the middle of the century, by contrast, all roads that would lead home must do so by way of *scriptura*. That, at least, is the truth as preached by Hugh Latimer, influential advocate of Church reform under Henry VIII and Edward VI, martyred under Mary Tudor in 1555. Despite the differences in their reading materials, their nationalities, and even their religions, however, Latimer keeps company with Montaigne in echoing suggestively and in the vernacular the pervasiveness of the largely Latin tradition considered here.

In answer to those who would argue that salvation comes through baptism, citing John 3:3, Latimer, fighting Scripture with Scripture, counters with 1 Peter 1:23. "It is not to be Christened in water . . . and nothyng elles . . . ," he claims, "[but b]y the word of the liuyng God, by the worde of God preached and opened."[4] Not content to make his point about achieving salvation through understanding God's word, Latimer offers in addition a hermeneutics for achieving this understanding: "That one place of Scripture declareth another. It is the circumstance, and collation of places that make scripture playne" (23).[5] In one sense, this book provides an extended gloss on Latimer's brief formulation of his exegetical method, demonstrating, along the way, Montaigne's observations on the inventive aspects of all glossing. For read in the light of the previous chapters, this formulation does little more with its "circumstance" and "collation of places" than render in English the *circumstantiae* and *collatio locorum* that we have seen to figure so prominently in the Latin manuals of Augustine, Erasmus, Melanchthon, and Flacius.

Understood in the context of his predecessors and contemporaries, that is, Latimer both practices and preaches the resolution of obscurity in Scripture by contextualizing difficult or ambiguous passages historically and textually. As we well know, these interpretive principles form the basis of

4. Hugh Latimer, "A Cure for Violence and Corruption: The Sixth Sermon Preached before King Edward VI the 12 Daye of April 1549," in *In God's Name: Examples of Preaching in England from the Act of Supremacy to the Act of Uniformity, 1534–1662*, edited by John Chandos (Indianapolis, 1971), 23. Cf. *The Works of Hugh Latimer*, vol. 1, edited by Rev. George Elwes Corrie, The Parker Society (Cambridge, 1844), 202.

5. See also *Serm. Septuag. Sunday* (1552), cited in the *Oxford English Dictionary* under *scope*, where Latimer recalls Melanchthon's discussion in the *Elements* of the relation between *status* and *scopus* (above, 83–85): "Euery parable hath *certum statum*, a certayne scope, . . . it is enough for vs when we haue the meaning of the principall scope, and more needeth not."

the hermeneutical theory of subsequent centuries—theory written increasingly in the vernacular. As I have claimed in the Introduction and detailed in the foregoing chapters, moreover, the evolution of these principles is unthinkable apart from *decorum* and *oeconomia* and the adversarial strategies developed to constitute meaning in the rhetorical (and, up through the sixteenth century, largely Latin) tradition of interpretation.

Bibliography of Secondary Sources

Aldridge, John William. *The Hermeneutics of Erasmus*. Richmond, 1966.

Alexander, Werner. *Hermeneutica Generalis: Zur Konzeption und Entwicklung der allgemeinem Verstehenslehre im 17 und 18 Jahrhundert*. Stuttgart, 1993.

Asmis, Elizabeth. "Philodemus's Poetic Theory and *On the Good King According to Homer*." *Classical Antiquity* 10 (1991): 1–45.

Baldwin, Charles Sears. *Medieval Rhetoric and Poetic*. New York, 1928.

Bate, H. N. "Some Technical Terms of Greek Exegesis." *Journal of Theological Studies* 24 (1923): 59–66.

Bedouelle, Guy. "The Consultations of the Universities and Scholars Concerning the 'Great Matter' of King Henry VIII." In *The Bible in the Sixteenth Century*, edited by David C. Steinmetz. Durham, 1990.

Béné, Charles. *Erasme et Saint Augustin, ou l'influence de Saint Augustin sur l'humanisme d'Erasme*. Geneva, 1969.

Bentley, Jerry H. *Humanists and Holy Writ: New Testament Scholarship in the Renaissance*. Princeton, 1983.

Bonner, Stanley F. *Education in Ancient Rome*. Berkeley, 1977.

———. *Roman Declamation in the Late Republic and Early Empire*. Liverpool, 1949.

Bouyer, Louis. "Erasmus in Relation to the Medieval Biblical Tradition." In *The Cambridge History of the Bible*, vol. 2. Cambridge, Mass., 1969, 492–505.

Boyle, Marjorie O'Rourke. *Erasmus on Language and Method in Theology*. Toronto, 1977.

———. *Rhetoric and Reform: Erasmus' Civil Dispute with Luther*. Cambridge, Mass., 1983.

Brann, Noel L. "Humanism and Germany." In *Renaissance Humanism: Foundations, Forms, and Legacy*, vol. 2, edited by Albert Rabil, Jr. Philadelphia, 1988.

Breen, Quirinus. "The terms 'Loci Communes' and 'Loci' in Melanchthon." *Christianity and Humanism: Studies in the History of Ideas*. Grand Rapids, 1968.

Bright, Pamela. *The Book of Rules of Tyconius: Its Purpose and Inner Logic*. Notre Dame, 1988.

Brown, Peter. *Augustine of Hippo*. Berkeley, 1967.

Bruns, Gerald L. *Hermeneutics Ancient and Modern*. New Haven, 1992.

———. "The Problem of Figuration in Antiquity." In *Hermeneutics: Questions and Prospects*, edited by Gary Shapiro and Alan Sica. Amherst, 1984.

Budiša, Dražen. "Humanism in Croatia." Translated by Ivo Banac. In *Renaissance Humanism: Foundations, Forms, and Legacy*, vol. 2, edited by Albert Rabil, Jr. Philadelphia, 1988.

Camporeale, Salvatore I. *Lorenzo Valla: Umanesimo e Teologia*. Florence, 1972.

Carruthers, Mary J. *The Book of Memory: A Study of Memory in Medieval Culture*. Cambridge, 1990.

Cave, Terence. *The Cornucopian Text: Problems of Writing in the French Renaissance*. Oxford, 1977.

Chomarat, Jacques. "Les *Annotations* de Valla, celles d'Erasme et la grammaire." *Histoire de l'exégèse au XVIe siècle*, edited by O. Fatio and P. Fraenkel. Geneva, 1978.

—. *Grammaire et rhéorique chez Erasme*. 2 vols. Paris, 1981.

—. "Grammar and Rhetoric in the Paraphrases of the Gospels by Erasmus." *Erasmus of Rotterdam Society Yearbook* 1 (1981): 30–68.

Cohen, Boaz. *Jewish and Roman Law*. New York, 1966.

—. "Letter and Spirit in Jewish and Roman Law." In *Mordecai M. Kaplan Jubilee Volume*, edited by Moshe Davis. New York, 1953.

—. "Note on Letter and Spirit in the New Testament." *Harvard Theological Review* 47 (1954): 197–203.

Colson, F. H. "The Grammatical Chapters in Quintilian 1.4–8." *Classical Quarterly* 8 (1914): 33–47.

Copeland, Rita. *Rhetoric, Hermeneutics and Translation in the Middle Ages: Academic Traditions and Vernacular Texts*. Cambridge, 1991.

Coulter, James. *The Literary Microcosm: Theories of Interpretation of the Later Neoplatonists*. Leiden, 1976.

Dale, A. M. "Ethos and Dianoia: 'Character' and 'Thought' in Aristotle's *Poetics*." In *Collected Papers*. Cambridge, 1969.

Dawson, David. *Allegorical Readers and Cultural Revision in Ancient Alexandria*. Berkeley, 1992.

Daube, David. "Alexandrian Methods of Interpretation and the Rabbis." In *Essays in Greco-Roman and Related Talmudic Literature*, edited by Henry A. Fischel. New York, 1977.

—. "Rabbinic Methods of Interpretation and Hellenistic Rhetoric." *Hebrew Union College Annual* 22 (1949): 239–64.

—. "Texts and Interpretation in Roman and Jewish Law." In *Essays in Greco-Roman and Related Talmudic Literature*, edited by Henry A. Fischel. New York, 1977.

Devereux, E. J. *Renaissance English Translations of Erasmus*. Toronto, 1983.

Dieter, Otto Alvin Loeb. "Stasis." *Speech Monographs* 17, no. 4 (1950): 345–69.

Dihle, Albrecht. *The Theory of Will in Classical Antiquity*. Berkeley, 1982.

Dilthey, Wilhelm. *Gesammelte Schriften*. Vol. 2. Leipzig, 1942.

—. "The Rise of Hermeneutics." Translated by Fredric Jameson. *New Literary History* 3 (1972): 229–44.

Dronke, Peter. *Fabula: Explorations into the Uses of Myth in Medieval Platonism.* Leiden, 1974.

Duchatelez, K. "La notion d'économie et ses richesses théologiques." *Nouvelle revue théologique* 92 (1970): 267–92.

Ebeling, Gerhard. *The Word of God and Tradition.* Translated by S. H. Hooke. London, 1968.

Eden, Kathy. "Economy in the Hermeneutics of Late Antiquity." In *Reconfiguring the Relation Rhetoric/Hermeneutics,* ed. George Pullman, *Studies in the Literary Imagination* 28 (1995): 13–26.

———. "Equity and the Origins of Renaissance Historicism: The Case for Erasmus." *Yale Journal of Law and the Humanities* 5 (1993): 137–45.

———. "Hermeneutics and the Ancient Rhetorical Tradition." *Rhetorica* 5 (1987): 59–86.

———. *Poetic and Legal Fiction in the Aristotelian Tradition.* Princeton, 1986.

———. "Rhetoric in the Hermeneutics of Erasmus' Later Works." *Erasmus of Rotterdam Society Yearbook* 11 (1991): 88–104.

———. "The Rhetorical Tradition and Augustinian Hermeneutics in *De doctrina christiana.*" *Rhetorica* 8 (1990): 45–63.

Erickson, John H. "*Oikonomia* in Byzantine Canon Law." In *Law, Church, and Society: Essays in Honor of Stephen Kuttner,* edited by Kenneth Pennington and Robert Somerville. Philadelphia, 1977.

Fedwick, Paul Jonathan. "A Chronology of the Life and Works of Basil of Caesarea." In *Basil of Caesarea, Christian, Humanist, Ascetic: A Sixteen-Hundredth Anniversary Symposium,* vol. 1, edited by Paul Jonathan Fedwick. Toronto, 1981.

Forbes, P. B. R. "Greek Pioneers in Philology and Grammar." *Classical Review* 47 (1933): 105–12.

Fortin, Ernest L. "Christianity and Hellenism in Basil the Great's Address *Ad Adulescentes.*" In *Neoplatonism and Early Christian Thought: Essays in Honor of A. H. Armstrong,* edited by H. J. Blumenthal and R. A. Markus. London, 1981.

Frede, Dorothea. "The Impossibility of Perfection: Socrates' Criticism of Simonides' Poem in the *Protagoras.*" *Review of Metaphysics* 39 (1986): 729–53.

Frede, Michael. *Essays in Ancient Philosophy.* Minneapolis, 1987.

Froehlich, Karlfried. "Always to Keep the Literal Sense in Holy Scripture Means to Kill One's Soul: The State of Biblical Hermeneutics at the Beginning of the Fifteenth Century." In *Literary Uses of Typology from the Latin Middle Ages to the Present,* edited by Earl Miner. Princeton, 1977.

Gadamer, Hans-Georg. *Truth and Method.* Translated by Joel Weinsheimer and Donald G. Marshall. New York, 1989.

———. *Dialogue and Dialectic: Eight Hermeneutical Studies on Plato.* Translated by P. Christopher Smith. New Haven, 1980.

———. *The Relevance of the Beautiful and Other Essays.* Translated by Nicholas Walker. Cambridge, 1986.

————. "Rhetorik und Hermeneutik." In *Gesammelte Werke.* Vol. 2. Tübingen, 1986.

Gilbert, Neal W. "The Concept of Will in Early Latin Philosophy." *Journal of the History of Philosophy* 1 (1963): 32–33.

Grafton, Anthony, and Lisa Jardine. *From Humanism to the Humanities: Education and the Liberal Arts in Fifteenth- and Sixteenth-Century Europe.* Cambridge, Mass., 1986.

————. "'Studied for Action': How Gabriel Harvey Read His Livy." *Past and Present* 129 (November 1990): 30–78.

Gray, Hanna H. "Renaissance Humanism: The Pursuit of Eloquence." *JHI* 24 (1963): 497–514.

Greene, T. M. *The Light in Troy.* New Haven, 1982.

Grondin, Jean. *Introduction to Philosophical Hermeneutics.* Translated by Joel Weinsheimer. New Haven, 1994.

Gundert, Hermann. "Die Simonides-Interpretation in Platons Protagoras." *EPMHNEIA: Festschrift Otto Regenbogen.* Heidelberg, 1952.

Gyeyke, K. "Aristotle on Language and Meaning." *International Philosophical Quarterly* 14 (1974): 71–77.

Halleux, André de. "'Oikonomia' in the First Canon of Saint Basil." *Patristic and Byzantine Review* 6 (1987): 53–64.

Halliwell, Stephen. *Aristotle's Poetics.* Chapel Hill, 1986.

Hamburger, Max. *The Awakening of Western Legal Thought.* Translated by Bernard Miall. London, 1942.

Heath, Malcolm. *Unity in Greek Poetics.* Oxford, 1989.

Herrick, Marvin T. *Comic Theory in the Sixteenth Century.* Illinois Studies in Language and Literature 34. Urbana, 1950.

Heubeck, Alfred, et al., eds. *A Commentary on Homer's Odyssey.* 3 vols. Oxford, 1988–92.

Hoffman, Manfred. "Erasmus on Language and Interpretation." *Moreana* 28 (1991): 3–20.

————. *Rhetoric and Theology: The Hermeneutic of Erasmus.* Toronto, 1994.

Hoy, David Couzens. *The Critical Circle: Literature, History and Philosophical Hermeneutics.* Berkeley, 1978.

Hunt, R. W. "The Introduction to the 'Artes' in the Twelfth Century." In *The History of Grammar in the Middle Ages,* edited by G. L. Bursill-Hall. Amsterdam, 1980.

Huxley, G. L. "Historical Criticism in Aristotle's *Homeric Questions.*" *Proceedings of the Royal Irish Academy* 79 (1979): 73–81.

Hyde, Michael J., and Craig Smith. "Hermeneutics and Rhetoric: A Seen but Unobserved Relationship." *Quarterly Journal of Speech* 65 (1979): 347–63.

Irvine, Martin. *The Making of Textual Culture: 'Grammatica' and Literary Theory, 350–1100.* Cambridge, 1994.

Irwin, T. H. "Aristotle's Concept of Signification." In *Language and Logos: Stud-*

ies in Ancient Greek Philosophy Presented to G. E. L. Owen, edited by Malcolm Schofield and Martha Craven Nussbaum. Cambridge, 1982.

Jonge, H. J. de. *"Novum testamentum a nobis versum:* The Essence of Erasmus' Edition of the New Testament." *Journal of Theological Studies* 35 (1984): 394–413.

Jordan, William J. "Aristotle's Concept of Metaphor in Rhetoric." In *Aristotle: The Classical Heritage of Rhetoric,* edited by Keith V. Erickson. Metuchen, N.J., 1974.

Kolb, Robert. "Teaching the Text: The Commonplace Method in Sixteenth-Century Lutheran Biblical Commentary." *Bibliothèque d'Humanisme et Renaissance* 49 (1987): 571–85.

Kaster, Robert A. *Guardians of Language: The Grammarian and Society in Late Antiquity.* Berkeley, 1988.

Keen, Ralph. *A Checklist of Melanchthon Imprints through 1560.* St. Louis, 1988.

Kelley, Donald R. "Civil Science in the Renaissance: The Problem of Interpretation." In *The Languages of Political Theory in Early-Modern Europe,* edited by A. Pagden. Cambridge, 1987.

———. *Foundations of Modern Historical Scholarship.* New York, 1970.

———. "Gaius Noster: Substructures of Western Social Thought." *American Historical Review* 84 (1979): 619–48.

———. "Hermes, Clio, Themis: Historical Interpretation and Legal Hermeneutics." *Journal of Modern History* 55 (1983): 644–68.

Kennedy, George A. *The Art of Rhetoric in the Roman World.* Princeton, 1972.

———. *Classical Rhetoric and Its Christian and Secular Tradition.* Chapel Hill, 1950.

———. *Greek Rhetoric under Christian Emperors.* Princeton, 1983.

Kinney, Daniel. ed. *The Complete Works of St. Thomas More.* Vol. 15. New Haven, 1986.

Kisch, Guido. *Erasmus und die Jurisprudenz seiner Zeit.* Basel, 1960.

———. *Gestalten und Probleme aus Humanismus und Jurisprudenz.* Berlin, 1969.

Kretzmann, Norman. "Aristotle on Spoken Sound Significant by Convention." In *Ancient Logic and Its Modern Interpretations,* edited by John Corcoran. Dordrecht, 1974.

Kurke, Leslie. *The Traffic in Praise: Pindar and the Poetics of Social Economy.* Ithaca, 1991.

Kuspit, D. B. "Melanchthon and Dürer: The Search for the Simple Style." *Journal of Medieval and Renaissance Studies* 3 (1973): 177–202.

Kustas, George L. "Saint Basil and the Rhetorical Tradition." In *Basil of Caesarea, Christian, Humanist, Ascetic: A Sixteen-Hundredth Anniversary Symposium,* vol. 1, edited by Paul Jonathan Fedwick. Toronto, 1981.

———. *Studies in Byzantine Rhetoric.* Thessaloniki, 1973.

Lamberton, Robert. *Homer the Theologian: Neoplatonic Allegorical Reading and the Growth of the Epic Tradition.* Berkeley, 1986.

———. "The Neoplatonists and the Spiritualization of Homer." In *Homer's Ancient Readers: The Hermeneutics of Greek Epic's Earliest Exegetes,* edited by Robert Lamberton and John J. Keaney. Princeton, 1992.

Lausberg, Heinrich. *Handbuch der Literarischen Rhetorik*. Munich, 1960.

Lewalski, Barbara Keifer. *Protestant Poetics and the Seventeenth-Century Religious Lyric*. Princeton, 1979.

Lim, Richard. "The Politics of Interpretation in Basil of Caesarea's *Hexaemeron*." *Vigiliae Christianae* 44 (1990): 351–70.

Long, A. A. "Stoic Readings of Homer." In *Homer's Ancient Readers: The Hermeneutics of Greek Epic's Earliest Exegetes*, edited by Robert Lamberton and John J. Keaney. Princeton, 1992.

Maclean, Ian. *Interpretation and Meaning in the Renaissance: The Case of Law*. Cambridge, 1992.

———. "The Place of Interpretation: Montaigne and Humanist Jurists on Words, Intention and Meaning." In *Neo-Latin and the Vernacular in Renaissance France*, edited by Grahame Caster and Terence Cave. Oxford, 1984.

Makkreel, Rudolf A. *Dilthey: Philosopher of the Human Studies*. Princeton, 1975.

Markus, R. A. "Trinitarian Theology and the Economy." *Journal of Theological Studies*, n.s., 9 (1958): 89–102.

Marrou, Henri-Irénée. *A History of Education in Antiquity*. Translated by George Lamb. New York, 1956.

———. *Saint Augustin et la fin de la culture antique*. Paris, 1938.

Maurer, Wilhelm. *Der Junge Melanchthon*. Vol. 1. Göttingen, 1967.

McConica, J. K. *Erasmus*. Oxford, 1991.

———. "Erasmus and the Grammar of Consent." In *Scrinium Erasmianum*, vol. 2, edited by J. Coppens. Leiden, 1969.

Meijering, Roos. *Literary and Rhetorical Theories in Greek Scholia*. Groningen, 1987.

Miller, A. M. "*Inventa componere*: Rhetorical Process and Poetic Composition in Pindar's Ninth Olympian Ode." *TAPA* 123 (1993): 109–47.

Minnis, A. J. *Medieval Theory of Authorship*. 2d ed. Philadelphia, 1988.

Moffatt, Ann. "The Occasion of St. Basil's *Address to Young Men*." *Antichton* 6 (1972): 83–86.

Monfasani, John. "Humanism and Rhetoric." In *Renaissance Humanism: Foundations, Forms, and Legacy*, vol. 3, edited by Albert Rabil, Jr. Philadelphia, 1988.

Most, Glenn W. "Rhetorik und Hermeneutik: Zur Konstitution Neuzeitlichkeit." *Antike und Abendland* 30 (1984): 62–79.

Murphy, James J. *Rhetoric in the Middle Ages*. Berkeley, 1974.

———. "Saint Augustine and the Debate about a Christian Rhetoric." *Quarterly Journal of Speech* 46 (1960): 400–410.

Nadeau, Ray. "Classical Systems of Stasis in Greek: Hermagoras to Hermogenes." *Greek, Roman, and Byzantine Studies* 2, no. 1 (1959): 51–71.

———. "Hermogenes' *On Stases*: A Translation with an Introduction and Notes." *Speech Monographs* 31, no. 4 (1964): 361–424.

Oberman, Heiko A. "Three Sixteenth-Century Attitudes Toward Judaism: Reuchlin, Erasmus and Luther." In *The Impact of the Reformation*. Grand Rapids, 1994.

Olson, Oliver K. *Shapers of Religious Tradition in Germany, Switzerland, and Poland, 1560–1600.* New Haven, 1981.

O'Malley, John W. "Content and Rhetorical Forms in Sixteenth-Century Treatises on Preaching." In *Renaissance Eloquence: Studies in the Theory and Practice of Renaissance Rhetoric,* edited by James J. Murphy. Berkeley, 1983.

————. "Erasmus and the History of Sacred Rhetoric: The *Ecclesiastes* of 1535." *Erasmus of Rotterdam Society Yearbook* 5 (1985): 1–29.

————. "Grammar and Rhetoric in the *pietas* of Erasmus." *Journal of Medieval and Renaissance Studies* 18 (1988): 81–98.

Orsy, Ladislas. "In Search of the Meaning of *Oikonomia*: Report on a Convention." *Theological Studies* 43 (1982): 312–19.

Padley, G. A. *Grammatical Theory in Western Europe, 1500–1700.* Cambridge, 1976.

Paré, G., A. Brunet, and P. Tremblay. *La Renaissance du XIIe siècle.* Paris, 1933.

Payne, John B. "Erasmus and Lefèvre d'Etaples as Interpreters of Paul." *Archiv für Reformationsgeschichte* 65 (1974): 54–83.

————. *Erasmus: His Theology of the Sacraments.* Richmond, 1970.

————. "Toward the Hermeneutics of Erasmus." In *Scrinium Erasmianum,* vol. 2, edited by J. Coppens. Leiden, 1969.

Pelikan, Jaroslav. *The Christian Tradition: A History of the Development of Doctrine.* Vol. 1. Chicago, 1971.

————. *Christianity and Classical Culture: The Metamorphosis of Natural Theology in the Christian Encounter with Hellenism.* New Haven, 1993.

————. "The 'Spiritual Sense' of Scripture." In *Basil of Caesarea, Christian, Humanist, Ascetic: A Sixteen-Hundredth Anniversary Symposium,* vol. 1, edited by Paul Jonathan Fedwick. Toronto, 1981.

Pfeiffer, Rudolf. *History of Classical Scholarship from the Beginnings to the End of the Hellenistic Age.* Oxford, 1968.

————. *History of Classical Scholarship from 1300 to 1850.* Oxford, 1976.

Piaget, Jean. *The Construction of Reality in the Child.* Translated by Margaret Cook. New Haven, 1954.

Pigman, G. W., III. "Imitation and the Renaissance Sense of the Past: The Reception of Erasmus' *Ciceronianus.*" *Journal of Medieval and Renaissance Studies* 9 (1979): 155–77.

Porter, James I. "Hermeneutic Lines and Circles: Aristarchus and Crates on the Exegesis of Homer." In *Homer's Ancient Readers: The Hermeneutics of Greek Epic's Earliest Exegetes,* edited by Robert Lamberton and John J. Keaney. Princeton, 1992.

Press, Gerald A. *The Development of the Idea of History in Antiquity.* Montreal, 1982.

————. "*Doctrina* in Augustine's *De doctrina christiana.*" *Philosophy and Rhetoric* 17 (1984): 98–115.

————. "The Subject and Structure of Augustine's *De doctrina christiana.*" *Augustiniana* 31 (1981): 165–82.

Prestige, G. L. *God in Patristic Thought.* London, 1952.

Preus, James Samuel. *From Shadow to Promise: Old Testament Interpretation from Augustine to the Young Luther.* Cambridge, Mass., 1969.

Quain, Edwin A. "The Medieval Accessus ad Auctores." *Traditio* 3 (1945): 215–64.

Reumann, John. "οἰκονομία as 'Ethical Accommodation' in the Fathers, and Its Pagan Background." *Studia Patristica* 3 (1961): 370–79.

————. "OIKONOMIA-terms in Paul in Comparison with Lucan *Heilsgeschichte.*" *New Testament Studies* 13 (1966–67): 147–67.

————. "The 'Righteousness of God' and the 'Economy of God': Two Great Doctrinal Themes Historically Compared." *A Festschrift for Archbishop Methodios of Thyateira and Great Britain.* Thyateira, 1985.

Richardson, N. J. "Aristotle's Reading of Homer and Its Background." In *Homer's Ancient Readers: The Hermeneutics of Greek Epic's Earliest Exegetes,* edited by Robert Lamberton and John J. Keaney. Princeton, 1992.

————. "Homeric Professors in the Age of the Sophists." *PCPS* 21 (1975): 65–81.

————. "Literary Criticism in the Exegetical Scholia to the *Iliad:* A Sketch." *Classical Quarterly* 30 (1980): 265–87.

Rist, John M. "Basil's 'Neoplatonism': Its Background and Nature." In *Basil of Caesarea, Christian, Humanist, Ascetic: A Sixteen-Hundredth Anniversary Symposium,* vol. 1, edited by Paul Jonathan Fedwick. Toronto, 1981.

Robertson, D. W., Jr. "A Note on the Classical Origin of 'Circumstances' in the Medieval Confessional." *Studies in Philology* 43 (1946): 6–14.

Robins, R. H. "Dionysius Thrax and the Western Grammatical Tradition." *Transactions of the Philological Society* (1957): 67–106.

Rosenmeyer, Thomas G. "Design and Execution in Aristotle, Poetics ch. XXV." *California Studies in Classical Antiquity* 6 (1973): 231–52.

Rummel, Erika. *Erasmus and His Catholic Critics.* Vol. 1. Nieuwkoop, 1989.

————. *Erasmus' Annotations on the New Testament.* Toronto, 1986.

————. "God and Solecism: Erasmus as a Literary Critic of the Bible." *Erasmus of Rotterdam Society Yearbook* 7 (1987): 54–72.

————. "St. Paul in Plain Latin: Erasmus' Philological Annotations on I Corinthians." *Classical and Modern Literature* 7 (1987): 309–18.

Russell, D. A. *Criticism in Antiquity.* London, 1981.

————. *Plutarch.* London, 1973.

Schaeublin, Christoph. "Homerum ex Homero." *Museum Helveticum* 34 (1977): 221–27.

Schanze, Helmut. "Problems and Trends in the History of German Rhetoric to 1500." *Renaissance Eloquence: Studies in the Theory and Practice of Renaissance Rhetoric.* Edited by James J. Murphy. Berkeley, 1983.

Schenkeveld, D. M. "The Structure of Plutarch's *De audiendis poetis.*" *Mnemosyne* 35 (1982): 60–71.

Schiffman, Zachary Sayre. *On the Threshold of Modernity: Relativism in the French Renaissance.* Baltimore, 1991.

————. "Renaissance Historicism Reconsidered." *History and Theory* 24 (1985): 170–82.

Schiller, Arthur A. "Roman Interpretatio and Anglo-American Interpretation and Construction." *Virginia Law Review* 27 (1941): 735–68.

————. *Roman Law*. The Hague, 1978.

Schneider, John. *Philip Melanchthon's Rhetorical Construal of Biblical Authority: Oratio Sacra*. Lewiston, N.Y., 1990.

Schottenloher, Otto. "Lex Naturae und Lex Christi bei Erasmus." In *Scrinium Erasmianum*, vol. 2, edited by J. Coppens. Leiden, 1969.

Segal, Alan F. *Paul the Convert*. New Haven, 1990.

Segal, Charles. "Bard and Audience in Homer." In *Homer's Ancient Readers: The Hermeneutics of Greek Epic's Earliest Exegetes*, edited by Robert Lamberton and John J. Keaney. Princeton, 1992.

Shuger, Debora. "Morris Croll, Flacius Illyricus, and the Origins of Anti-Ciceronianism." *Rhetorica* 3 (1985): 269–84.

————. *The Renaissance Bible: Scholarship, Sacrifice, and Subjectivity*. Berkeley, 1994.

Sider, Robert Dick. *Ancient Rhetoric and the Art of Tertullian*. Oxford, 1971.

————. "Concedo nulli: Erasmus' Motto and the Figure of Paul in the Paraphrases." *Erasmus in English* 14 (1985–86): 7–10.

Smalley, Beryl. *The Study of the Bible in the Middle Ages*. Oxford, 1952.

Snyder, Jane McIntosh. "The Web of Song: Weaving Imagery in Homer and the Lyric Poets." *Classical Journal* 76 (1980–81): 193–96.

Solmsen, Friedrich. "The Aristotelian Tradition in Ancient Rhetoric." *AJP* 62 (1941): 35–50, 169–90.

Spitz, Lewis. "Humanism and the Protestant Reformation." In *Renaissance Humanism: Foundations, Forms, and Legacy*, vol. 3, edited by Albert Rabil, Jr. Philadelphia, 1988.

Spitzer, Leo. *Linguistics and Literary Theory*. Princeton, 1948.

Stanford, William Bedell. *Ambiguity in Greek Literature*. Oxford, 1939.

Stroux, Johannes. *Summum ius summa iniuria, ein Kapitel aus der Geschichte der interpretatio iuris*. Basel, 1926.

Struever, Nancy. *The Language of History in the Renaissance*. Princeton, 1970.

Szondi, Peter. "Introduction to Literary Hermeneutics." Translated by Timothy Bahti. *New Literary History* 10 (1978): 17–28.

Telle, Emile V. "Erasmus's *Ciceronianus*: A Comical Colloquy." In *Essays on the Works of Erasmus*, edited by Richard L. DeMolen. New Haven, 1978.

Thomson, Wayne N. "Stasis in Aristotle's *Rhetoric*." *Quarterly Journal of Speech* 58 (1972): 134–41.

Todorov, Tzvetan. "The Birth of Occidental Semiotics." *The Sign: Semiotics around the World*, edited by R. W. Bailey, L. Matejka, and P. Steiner. Ann Arbor, 1978.

————. *Symbolism and Interpretation*. Translated by Catherine Porter. Ithaca, 1982.

Trimpi, Wesley. "Horace's 'Ut Pictura Poesis': The Argument for Stylistic Decorum." *Traditio* 34 (1978): 29–73.

———. "The Meaning of Horace's *Ut Pictura Poesis.*" *Journal of the Warburg and Courtauld Institutes* 36 (1973): 1–34.

———. *Muses of One Mind: The Literary Analysis of Experience and Its Continuity.* Princeton, 1983.

———. "Reason and the Classical Premises of Literary Decorum." *Independent Journal of Philosophy* 5/6 (1988): 103–11.

Trinkaus, Charles E. "Erasmus, Augustine and the Nominalists." *Archiv für Reformationsgeschichte* 67 (1976): 5–32.

———. *In Our Image and Likeness.* 2 vols. Chicago, 1970.

Tsirpanlis, Constantine N. "Doctrinal 'Oikonomia' and Sacramental Koinonia in Greek Patristic Theology and Contemporary Orthodox Ecumenism." *The Patristic and Byzantine Review* 6 (1987): 30–43.

Valgiglio, Ernesto. "Basilio Magno *Ad Adulescentes* e Plutarco *De audiendis poetis.*" *Rivista di studi classici* 23 (1975): 67–86.

Voegelin, Eric. *The Ecumenic Age.* Baton Rouge, 1974.

Ward, John O. "Renaissance Commentators on Ciceronian Rhetoric." In *Renaissance Eloquence,* edited by J. J. Murphy. Berkeley, 1983.

Warnke, Georgia. *Gadamer, Hermeneutics, Tradition and Reason.* Cambridge, 1987.

Weinsheimer, Joel. *Philosophical Hermeneutics and Literary Theory.* New Haven, 1991.

Weiss, James Michael. "*Ecclesiastes* and Erasmus: The Mirror and the Image." *Archiv für Reformationsgeschichte* 65 (1974): 83–108.

Wilson, N. G., ed. *St. Basil on the Value of Greek Literature.* London, 1975.

Young, David. "Pindar, Aristotle and Homer: A Study in Ancient Criticism." *Classical Antiquity* 2 (1983): 156–70.

Young, Frances. "The Rhetorical Schools and Their Influence on Patristic Exegesis." In *The Making of Orthodoxy: Essays in Honor of Henry Chadwick,* edited by Rowan Williams. Cambridge, 1989.

Zeitlin, Solomon. "Hillel and the Hermeneutic Rules." In *Studies in the Early History of Judaism.* Vol. 1. New York, 1973.

Index

About Yale Studies in Hermeneutics

Yale Studies in Hermeneutics provides a venue for inquiry into the theory of interpretation in all its varieties and domains. Titles in the series seek to expand and deepen our understanding of understanding while explicitly framing and situating themselves within the tradition of recognized hermeneutical thinkers from antiquity to the present.

[Handwritten notes:]

oeconomia

artificial org⁻, onomeo emotion, 11 to social orgs⁻ of family : structured to make one feel at home
WHAT is the connection ē club culture of science?
→ is it purely that science is unaware of the artifice?
or science works ē proof where no = vorba for a pre-agreed set of understandings. This is a quite diff. org⁻ of reaching a set of understandings that allow belief by being emotive, artificial arguments.

Plutarch reads Homer's Odyssey as tale abt weaving tales, tale about due travels needed to effect the recommod⁻ ē necessary to return travel, ie the relation need for accommod⁻ to make fittingly familiar.
[our readings of the Odyssey not only inform the Homeric ē all the later use of the Homeric]

Basil's oeconomic strategies, esp. at time of ecumenism
→ ecumenism also related to oikos or family
[what is role of dvdt⁻ēm family?]

rhet: accomod⁻ ᵗᵒ d/u formation

p10 - interp^n : word & intention → proof & ambiguity → style.
[is it ambiguity or ambivalence]

+ Must as art of accommodation (14 & school)
Arist → Cicero & Quint^n : ability to read 'improscription' i.e. that which is
① not written down & intended for written djs... cannot speak for all
circumstances & all times.
∴ ② context : hist'l [negotium + decorum] + textual
  → easy to see intention if you look at the whole
- rhetoricians trained first in grammar of the reading of poetry (20)
  - adversarial - e.g. Soc. refuting over the interp^n of an ode. (21-22)
  - on metaphor (24 →) + 25-26 : no transl^n.
1) ⇒ epieikeia : equity → corrects by accommodating.
2) 26 : in style : to prepon (decorum) → to adapt oneself to fit all sizes
  → same for orator as for grammarian & poet
decorum is to rhetoric as hist'l context is to lit. interpret^n or recept^n
  → int. poetry is an historical investig^n
3) oikonomia : elocution or style in Gk & dispositio in both : accom^n to particular case
  oeconomia : indirect & artificial org^n vs. taxis or dispositio : stfwd org^n (28)
  " - arouses and. emotion.
  → oratorical economy thinks of the whole when deriving the parts.
    - unified multiplicity [29] || social org^n of family.
30) so oeconomia & decorum justify textual context & underlie hist'l context
  " → whole has priority ∴ || to equity in ethics
  → interpret^n : accommod^n or coming to feel at home, making familiar.
Plutarch's reading poetry ethically, correcting the text, learning to use one
  significance at one time & another on another.
  → must have decorum & oeconomia ☞ to prepon & to oikeion
  + → she trans. to prepon as propriety & to eikos as probability ✗
like _Plutarch considers fiction itself as an accommodation (34)[whereas] Aristotle
Plato carve out special strategies for fiction that are institutionalised by the grammarians
  into accommod^n.
34 - poetry mitigates the pain that comes ∴ 'sameness' of truth + exploits pleasure in variety
  ∴ = Arist. fiction / plot & wine , ō Plutarch poetry / plot = colour (variegation)
  → for Plutarch, poetry is ethical & formal - he rejects Stoic allegory BUT
    takes an allegory of reading.
  → Pl's reader moves to philos & grammar / poetry at same time.
                  ✗
Basil sees reading classics (poetry) as a prep^n for reading scripture.
  - & also like Plutarch, Basil sees interpret^n as Odysseus' struggle to get home
Augustine → power of accommod^n notch fiction & in X who is way & truth (rhet-phil)
  - to interpret scripture is to weave its meaning (54)
(55) - A. stresses need for hist'l context to resolve ambiguity (+ textual context)
  scriptum vs. voluntas → scriptura's (will of interpreter) is even the signatus interprets
  ⇒ [spiritual & carnal] readings.

St. Paul : scriptura & voluntas $\xrightarrow{Heb'd}$ gramma & pneuma $\xrightarrow{Grk}$ littera & spiritus.
- voluntas & spirity → equity & wholeness.
- wholeness of χ^2, is caritas vs. cupiditas, charity (equity)
→ must not stop @ the carnal or just @ the letter, must seek intention (58)
Aug. also look at literal & fig're language: reader must dist. bet. the two.
→ lit. is better than figural if it is in accord @ caritas of text.
∴ can read literally & not stop just @ the 'letter' } 2 diff. things.
& thus evade the fixity of Jewish readings & the allegorizing of the Greeks.
———H———

Erasmus continues trad= @a addo, in his devol= theological texts, & expands
on decorum, the notion of history.
- for Eras: spiritual + equitable + historicist reading means to interpret=
- dialogue bet. $\overset{A}{fixed}$ & $\overset{B}{decorous}$ " decorous writing
  [is this word/spirit (or) lit/allg'l?]
- B's argument foregrounds the chapter of time - ie. change of temporal context.
* p. 70 v. imp't bit abt. reassessing the grounds, or possibly behaving indeterm. ✗
- Erasmus warns against allegorisers who ignore history (71) + against fixed readrs
- wants a reading, original, familiar (at home), germane
- interpret= aims at meaning @ which writer & interpreter can be at home (73)
→ have to have context: in language & conf= of transl=

reconstruction: need'l imitation + Biblical hermeneutics. } same as Erasmus'
  writing   reading   (?)
- compos= & interpret= } complementary.
- both writers & readers can become lost travellers.
→ interpreting Paul ll imitating Cicero → finding the whole, hexis of Ciceronian
- follow several models & deviate when decorum requires.
- guiding principle of organisation → oikonomia ! & no hard & fast rules.
- ll to stasis in rhet's invention: the basic premise at heart of problem
  (negotie) or controversy. (83) → summa cause the heart of the matter
  → this is summa, fixes in voluntas. (scopus)
Mel. reads for summa (primary meaning) vs. 4-fold allegorical readings that
  multiply the meanings/sententiae of a text.
- 3 kinds of status — conjectural, legal, juridical (86) } see p86 for more.
87. → discrep. bet. scripture & voluntas shd be resolved by dialectical/proof
  → & ambiguity is sorted by grammar/poetry
  → so Mel. brings together reading & writing in rhet'l tradition
———H———

Protestant Hermeneutics: Flacius Clavis: simil. to Mel & Erasmus → Cic/Quint
→ the need to est. authorial intention → comes out. for 'context' is stable,
the anti-allegory drive is stronger that the anti-fixity, voluntas = propositum.
- text ≡ human body : parts in larger unity [χ^2] accomodat= @a myst=
  → uses Plato's the one & the many (Phaedrus) to argue for sum of parts & whole
- good writing has scopus ≡ body 'head/face in genres
- scopus of writing = voluntas of writer. BUT scopus is largely to do @
psychology of reader : must have experience in reading